Anonymous

The Politician's Creed

Vol. II

Anonymous

The Politician's Creed
Vol. II

ISBN/EAN: 9783337069322

Printed in Europe, USA, Canada, Australia, Japan

Cover: Foto ©Suzi / pixelio.de

More available books at **www.hansebooks.com**

THE

POLITICIAN's CREED;

OR,

POLITICAL EXTRACTS:

BEING

AN ANSWER TO THESE QUESTIONS,

What is the best Form of Government?

AND

What is the best Administration of a Government?

BY A LOVER OF SOCIAL ORDER.

VOL. II.

PHILOSOPHY consists not
In airy schemes, or idle speculations:
The rule and conduct of all social life
Is her great province. Not in lonely cells
Obscure she lurks, but holds her *heav'nly light*
To senates and to kings, to guide her councils,
And teach them to reform and bless mankind.
THOMSON.

LONDON:
Printed for ROBINSONS, Paternoster-Row; T. COX, St. Thomas's-street, Borough; DILLY in the Poultry; MURRAY and HIGHLEY, Fleet-street; RICHARDSON, Cornhill; WHITE, Fleet-street; BECKET, and EDWARDS, Pall Mall; HOOKHAM and CARPENTER, Bond-street; and H. D. SYMONDS, No. 20, Paternoster-Row.

1799.

PREFACE.

In the preceding Volume the Editor of The Politician's Creed has attempted to give *the essence* or *forms* of different Governments, and, as far as could be done, consistent with the general design of this work, to ascertain *our* MIXED FORM *of Government*.

In these we are not to consider, whence *power* is derived; but the *acts* of *Legislation:* not what *constitutes a Government*; but what are the *emanations* of *established Forms*.

The writer of The Politician's Creed wishes the reader carefully to discriminate between *Acts of Legiſlation* and *Forms of Government.*—Thus a *chancellor* may be corrupt, a *particular jury* may be prejudiced, a *miniſter* improvident, a *commander* indiſcreet; nevertheleſs theſe *offices* or *forms* are as much a ſubject of *admiration* as before.

As, on the one hand, *all parties* have approved *our* MIXED FORM *of Government,* and here our *political knowledge* was reduced to a *ſcience*; ſo on the other hand, as the *practical part* muſt depend much upon *circumſtances,* we ſee opened a wide and endleſs field for diſputation.

Some general maxims, however, concerning COMMERCE, TREATIES, TAXES, WAR, &c. are attempted, and *hereafter* theſe ſeveral ſections may be better filled up by ſome enlightened politician, whom the Editor wiſhes the *ſame motive,* that has guided him in this work—a bias to TRUTH, rather than to any prevailing party, and the heartfelt pleaſure of beſtowing the PROFITS on perſons deſerving of the firſt conſideration; it being intended that the profits of this work ſhould go to the fund for the relief of the widows and orphan children of thoſe brave men, who may die fighting for their king and country, during this war, againſt an ambitious power, that wiſhes to overſtride all Europe.

CONTENTS

OF

THE SECOND VOLUME.

SECT.

CONTENTS.

PART II.

POLITICAL DISQUISITIONS

ON

THE ADMINISTRATION

OF

GOVERNMENTS.

SECT. I.

OF THE BALANCE OF POWER.

It is a queſtion, whether the *idea* of THE BALANCE OF POWER be owing entirely to *modern policy*, or whether the *phraſe only* has been *invented* in *theſe latter ages?* It is certain, that XENOPHON *, in his Inſtitution of CYRUS, repreſents the combination of the ASIATIC powers to have ariſen from a jealouſy of the increaſing force of the MEDES and PERSIANS; and though that elegant compoſition ſhould be ſuppoſed altogether a romance, this ſentiment, aſcribed by the author to the *eaſtern princes*, is at leaſt a proof of the prevailing notion of ancient times.

In all the politics of GREECE, the anxiety, with regard to *the balance of power*, is apparent, and is expreſsly pointed out to us, even by the ancient hiſtorians. THUCYDIDES † repreſents the league, which was form-

* Lib. i. † Lib. i.

ed againſt *Athens*, and which produced the *Peloponneſian war*, as entirely owing to this principle.—And after the decline of *Athens*, when the *Thebans* and *Lacedemonians* diſputed for ſovereignty, we find, that the *Athenians* (as well as many other republics) always threw themſelves into the *lighter ſcale*, and *endeavoured to preſerve the balance.*—They ſupported *Thebes* againſt *Sparta*, till the great victory gained by EPAMINONDAS at *Leuctra*; after which they immediately went over to the conquered from generoſity, as they *pretended*, but, *in reality, from their jealouſy of the conquerors* *.

Whoever will read DEMOSTHENES's oration for the *Megalopolitans*, may ſee the utmoſt refinements on this principle, that ever entered into the head of a VENETIAN or ENGLISH ſpeculatiſt, and upon the firſt riſe of the *Macedonian power*, this orator immediately diſcovered the danger, *ſounded the alarm through all Greece*, and at laſt aſſembled that *confederacy* under the banners of *Athens*, which fought the great and deciſive battle of *Chaeronea*.

It is true, the GRECIAN wars are regarded by hiſtorians as wars of *emulation* rather than of *politics*; and each

* XENOPH. Hiſt. GRAEC. lib. vi. & vii.

ſtate

ate ſeems to have had more in view the honour of leading the reſt, than any well-grounded hopes of authority and dominion.—If we conſider, indeed, the ſmall number of inhabitants in any one republic, compared to the whole, the great difficulty of forming ſieges in thoſe times, and the extraordinary bravery and diſcipline of every freeman among that people; we ſhall conclude, that the balance of power was, of itſelf, ſufficiently ſecured in GREECE, and needed not to have been guarded with that caution which may be requiſite in other ages.—But whether to aſcribe the *ſhifting of ſides* in all the GRECIAN republics to *jealous emulation* or *cautious politics*, the effects were alike, and every *prevailing power* was ſure to meet with a *confederacy* againſt it, and that often compoſed of its *former friends* and *allies*.

The ſame principle, call it envy or prudence, which produced the OSTRACISM of *Athens*, and PETALISM of *Syracuſe*, and expelled every citizen whoſe fame or power overtopped the reſt; the ſame principle, I ſay, naturally diſcovered itſelf in foreign politics, and ſoon raiſed enemies to the *leading* ſtate, however moderate in the exerciſe of its authority.

The *Perſian monarch* was really, in his force, a petty prince, compared to the GRECIAN republics; and therefore it behoved him, from views of safety more than from emulation, to interest himself in their quarrels, and to support the weaker side in every contest.—This was the advice given by ALCIBIADES to TISSAPHERNES *, and it prolonged near a century the date of the PERSIAN empire; till the neglect of it for a moment, after the first appearance of the aspiring genius of PHILIP, brought that lofty and frail edifice to the ground, with a rapidity of which there are few instances in the history of mankind.

The successors of ALEXANDER showed great jealousy of *the balance of power*; a jealousy founded on true politics and prudence, and which preserved distinct for several ages the partitions made after the death of that famous conqueror.—The fortune and ambition of ANTIGONUS † threatened them anew with a universal monarchy; but their combination, and their victory at *Ipsus* saved them.—And in after times, we find, that, as the Eastern princes considered the *Greeks* and *Macedonians* as the only real military force, with whom they had any intercourse, they kept always a *watchful eye* over that part of the world.—The PTOLEMIES, in par-

* THUCYD. lib. viii.

† DIOD. SIC. lib. xx.

ticular,

ticular, ſupported firſt ARATUS and the *Achaeans*, and then CLEOMENES king of *Sparta*, from no other view than as a *counterbalance* to the *Macedonian monarchs*.—For this is the account which POLYBIUS gives of the *Egyptian politics**.

The reaſon, why it is ſuppoſed, that the ancients were entirely ignorant of *the balance of power*, ſeems to be drawn from the ROMAN hiſtory more than the GRECIAN; and as the tranſactions of the former are generally the moſt familiar to us, we have thence formed all our concluſions.—It muſt be owned, that the ROMANS never met with any ſuch general combination or confederacy againſt them, as might naturally have been expected from their rapid conqueſts and declared ambition; *but were allowed peaceably to ſubdue their neighbours, one after another, till they extended their dominion over the whole known world*.—Not to mention the fabulous hiſtory of their ITALIC wars; there was, upon HANNIBAL's invaſion of the ROMAN ſtate, a remarkable criſis, which ought to have called up the attention of all civilized nations.—It appeared afterwards (nor was it diffi-

* Lib. ii. cap. 51.

cult to be obſerved at the time)* that this was a conteſt for *univerſal empire*; and *yet* no prince or ſtate ſeems to have been in the leaſt alarmed about the event or iſſue of the quarrel.—PHILIP of *Macedon* remained neuter, till he ſaw the victories of HANNIBAL; and then moſt imprudently formed an alliance with the conqueror, upon terms ſtill more imprudent.—He ſtipulated, that he was to aſſiſt the *Carthaginian* ſtate in their conqueſt of *Italy*; after which they engaged to ſend over forces into *Greece*, to aſſiſt him in ſubduing the *Grecian commonwealths* †.

The *Rhodian* and *Achaean* republics are much celebrated by ancient hiſtorians for their wiſdom and ſound policy; yet both of them aſſiſted the *Romans* in their wars againſt PHILIP and ANTIOCHUS.—And what may be eſteemed ſtill a ſtronger proof, that this maxim was not *generally known* in thoſe ages; no ancient author has remarked the *imprudence of theſe meaſures*, nor has even blamed that *abſurd treaty* above mentioned, made by PHILIP with the *Carthaginians*.—Princes and ſtateſmen,

* It was obſerved by ſome, as appears by the ſpeech of AGELAUS of NAUPACTUM, in the general congreſs of GREECE. See POLYB. lib. v. cap. 104.

† TITI LIVII, lib. iii. cap. 33.

in

in all ages, may, *before-hand*, be blinded in their reaſonings with regard to events: but it is ſomewhat extraordinary, that hiſtorians, *afterwards*, ſhould not form a ſounder judgment of them.

MASSINISSA, ATTALUS, PRUSIAS, in gratifying their *private paſſions*, were, all of them, the inſtrument of the *Roman greatneſs*; and never ſeem to have ſuſpected, that they were forging their own chains, while they advanced the conqueſts of their ally.—A ſimple treaty and agreement between MASSINISSA and the *Carthaginians*, ſo much required by mutual intereſt, would have barred the *Romans* from all entrance into *Africa*, and preſerved liberty to mankind.

The only prince we met with in the ROMAN hiſtory, who ſeems to have underſtood *the balance of power*, is HIERO king of *Syracuſe*.—Though the ally of ROME, he ſent aſſiſtance to the CARTHAGINIANS, during the war of the auxiliaries; "*Eſteeming it requiſite,*" ſays POLYBIUS*, "*both in order to retain his dominions in* "*Sicily, and to preſerve the Roman friendſhip, that* CAR-"THAGE *ſhould be ſafe; leſt by its fall the remaining* "*power ſhould be able, without contraſt or oppoſition, to* "*execute every purpoſe and undertaking.—And here he*

* Lib. i. cap. 83.

"*acted*

" *acted with great wisdom and prudence.—For that is ne-*
" *ver, on any account, to be overlooked; nor ought such a*
" *force ever to be thrown into one hand, as to incapacitate*
" *the neighbouring states from defending their rights against*
" *it.*"—Here is the aim of MODERN POLITICS pointed out in express terms.

In short, the maxim of preserving *the balance of power* is founded so much on *common sense* and *obvious reasoning*, that it is impossible it could *altogether* have escaped antiquity, where we find in other particulars so many marks of deep penetration and discernment.—If it was not so *generally* known and acknowledged as *at present*, it had, at least, an influence on all the wiser and more experienced princes and politicians.—And indeed, even at present, however generally known and acknowledged among *speculative reasoners*, it has not, *in practice*, an authority much more extensive among those who govern the world.

After the fall of the ROMAN empire, the form of government, established by the northern conquerors, incapacitated them, in a great measure, for farther conquests, and long maintained each state in its proper boundaries.—But when vassalage and the feudal militia were abolished, mankind were anew alarmed by the danger of *universal monarchy*, from the union of ſo many kingdoms and principalities in the perſon of the emperor CHARLES.—But the power of the houſe of *Auſtria*, founded on extenſive but divided dominions, and their riches, derived chiefly from mines of gold and ſilver, were more likely to decay, of themſelves, from internal defects, than to overthrow all the bulwarks raiſed againſt them.—In leſs than a century, the force of that violent and haughty race was ſhattered, their opulence diſſipated, their ſplendor eclipſed.—*A new power ſucceeded*, more *formidable* to *the liberties* of EUROPE, poſſeſſing all the advantages of the former, and labouring under none of its defects; except a ſhare of that ſpirit of bigotry and perſecution, with which the houſe of AUSTRIA was ſo long infatuated.

In the general wars, maintained againſt *this ambitious power*, BRITAIN has ſtood *foremoſt*; and ſhe ſtill maintains her ſtation.—*Beſide advantages of riches and ſituation, her people are animated with ſuch a national ſpirit, and are ſo fully ſenſible of the bleſſings of their government, that we may hope their vigour never will languiſh in ſo neceſſary and ſo juſt a cauſe.*—On the contrary, if we may judge by the paſt, *their paſſionate ardour* ſeems rather to require ſome moderation; and they have oftener erred from a *laudable exceſs* than from a *blamable deficiency.*

These

These excesses, to which we have been carried, are *prejudicial*; and may, perhaps, in time, become *still more prejudical* another way, by begetting, as is usual, the *opposite extreme*, and rendering us totally *careless* and *supine* with regard to the *fate* of *our Neighbours*.—The *Athenians*, from the most bustling, intriguing, warlike people of GREECE, finding their *error* in thrusting themselves into every quarrel, *abandoned all attention to foreign affairs*; and in no contest, ever took part on either side, except by their flatteries and complaisance to the victor*.—They repented of this folly when it was too late.

UPON THE WHOLE IT APPEARS THEN, THAT ALLIANCES ARE PROPER, AND AS THE AMBITION OF EXTENSIVE DOMINION IS MORE PREDOMINANT IN THE BREASTS OF RULERS, THAN GENERAL PHILANTHROPY, WHICH WILL EVER BE THE CASE, AS LONG AS MANKIND PERSIST IN APPLAUDING THEIR DESTROYERS, RATHER THAN THEIR BENEFACTORS, NATIONS OUGHT TO HAVE A JEALOUS EYE ON EACH OTHER, AND TO CONFEDERATE TOGETHER TO SUPPRESS THE RISING FLAME OF INORDINATE AMBITION, WHICH OTHERWISE, LIKE THE CHARIOT OF PHAETON, MIGHT CONFLAGRATE THE WHOLE WORLD.

* Hume.

SECT.

SECT. II.

OF THE BALANCE OF TRADE.

It is very uſual, in nations *ignorant* of *the nature of commerce*, to prohibit the *exportation* of commodities, and to preſerve among themſelves whatever they think valuable and uſeful.—They do not conſider that, in this prohibition, they act directly *contrary* to *their intention*; and that the more is *exported* of any commodity, the more will be *raiſed at home*, of which they themſelves will always have the firſt offer.

It is well known to the learned, that the ancient laws of ATHENS rendered the *exportation* of figs criminal; that being ſuppoſed a ſpecies of fruit ſo excellent in ATTICA, that the ATHENIANS deemed it too delicious for the palate of any foreigner.—There are proofs in many old acts of parliament of the *ſame ignorance* in the nature of commerce, particularly in the reign of EDWARD III.—And to this day, in FRANCE, the exportation of *corn* is almoſt always prohibited; in order, as they ſay, to *prevent famines*; though it is evident, that *nothing contributes more to the frequent famines, which ſo much diſtreſs that fertile country.*

The ſame jealous fear, with regard to *money*, has alſo prevailed among ſeveral nations; and it required both reaſon and experience to convince any people, that theſe prohibitious ſerve to no other purpoſe than to raiſe the exchange againſt them, and produce a ſtill greater exportation.

Theſe errors, one may ſay, are groſs and palpable: But there ſtill prevails, even in nations well acquainted with commerce, a ſtrong jealouſy with regard to *the balance of trade*, and a fear, that all their gold and ſilver may be leaving them.—This ſeems to me, almoſt in every caſe, a groundleſs apprehenſion; and I ſhould as ſoon dread, that all our ſprings and rivers ſhould be exhauſted, as that money ſhould abandon a kingdom where there are people and induſtry.—Let us carefully preſerve *theſe latter advantages*; and we need never be apprehenſive of *loſing the former.*

It is eaſy to obſerve, that all calculations concerning the balance of trade are founded on very uncertain facts and ſuppoſitions.—The cuſtom-houſe books are allowed to be an inſufficient ground of reaſoning; nor is the

rate

rate of exchange much better; unless we consider it with all nations, and know also the proportions of the several sums remitted; which one may safely pronounce impossible. Every man, who has ever reasoned on this subject, has always proved his theory, whatever it was, by facts and calculations, and by an enumeration of all the commodities sent to all foreign kingdoms.

The writings of Mr. GEE *struck the nation with an universal panic, when they saw it plainly demonstrated, by a detail of particulars, that the balance was against them for so considerable a sum as must leave them without a single shilling in five or six years.—But luckily, twenty years have since elapsed, with an expensive foreign war; yet is it commonly supposed, that money is still more plentiful among us than in any former period.*

Nothing can be more entertaining on this head than Dr. SWIFT; an author so quick in discerning the mistakes and absurdities of others.—He says, in his *Short View of the State of* IRELAND, that the whole cash of that kingdom formerly amounted but to 500,000*l.*; that out of this the IRISH remitted every year a neat million to ENGLAND, and had scarcely any other source from which they could compensate themselves, and little other foreign trade than the importation of FRENCH wines, for which they paid ready money. The consequence of this situation, which must be owned to be disadvantageous, was, that, in a course of three years, the current money of IRELAND, from 500,000*l.* was reduced to less than two.—And at present, I suppose, in a course of 30 years, it is absolutely nothing.—Yet I know not how that opinion of the *advance of riches in* IRELAND, which gave the Doctor so much indignation, seems still to continue, and gain ground with every body.

In short, this apprehension of the wrong balance of trade, appears of such a nature, that it discovers itself, wherever one is *out of humour with the ministry, or is in low spirits*; and as it can never be refuted by a particular detail of all the exports, which counterbalance the imports, it may here be proper to form a general argument, that may prove the impossibility of this even, as long as we preserve our people and our industry.

Suppose four-fifths of all the money in BRITAIN *to be annihilated in one night, and the nation reduced to the same condition, with regard to specie, as in the reigns of the* HARRYS *and* EDWARDS, *what would be the consequence? Must not the price of all labour and commodities sink in*

 proportion,

proportion, and every thing be ſold as cheap as they were in thoſe ages?—What nation could then diſpute with us in any foreign market, or pretend to navigate or to ſell manufactures at the ſame price, which to us would afford ſufficient profit?—In how little time, therefore, muſt this bring back the money which we had loſt, and raiſe us to the level of all the neighbouring nations?—Where, after we have arrived, we immediately loſe the advantage of the cheapneſs of labour and commodities; and the farther flowing in of money is ſtopped by our fulneſs and repletion.*

Again, *ſuppoſe that all the money of* BRITAIN *were multiplied fivefold in a night, muſt not the contrary effect follow?—Muſt not all labour and commodities riſe to ſuch an exorbitant height, that no neighbouring nations could afford to buy from us; while their commodities, on the other hand, became comparatively ſo cheap, that, in ſpite of all the laws which could be formed, they would be run in upon us, and our money flow out; till we fall to a level with foreigners, and loſe that great ſuperiority of riches, which had laid us under ſuch diſadvantages.*

Now, it is evident, that the ſame cauſes, which would *correct* theſe exorbitant inequalities, were they to happen

* Like a poor man, we ſhould be able to *ſell* every thing, but *buy* nothing.

happen miraculoufly, muft prevent their happening in the common courfe of nature, and muft for ever, in all neighbouring nations, preferve money nearly proportionable to the art and induftry of each nation.—*All water, wherever it communicates, remains always at a level.*—Afk naturalifts the reafon; they tell you, that were it to be raifed in any one place, the fuperior gravity of that part not being balanced, muft deprefs it, till it meet a counterpoife; and that the fame caufe, which redreffes the inequality when it happens, muft for ever prevent it, without fome violent external operation.

Can one imagine that it had ever been poffible, by any laws, or even by any art or induftry, to have kept all the money in SPAIN, which the galleons have brought from the *Indies*?—Or that all commodities could be fold in FRANCE for a tenth of the price which they would yield on the other fide of the PYRENEES, without finding their way thither, and draining from that immenfe treafure?—What other reafon, indeed, is there, why all nations, at prefent, gain in their trade with SPAIN and PORTUGAL; but becaufe it is impoffible to heap up money, more than any fluid, beyond its proper level?—*The fovereigns of thefe countries have fhewn, that they wanted not inclination to keep their gold*

and

and ſilver to themſelves, had it been in any degree prac- ticeable.

But as any body of water may be raiſed above the level of the ſurrounding element, if the former has no communication with the latter; ſo in money, if the communication be cut off, by any material or phyſical impediment (for all laws alone are ineffectual), there may, in ſuch a caſe, be a very great inequality of money.—Thus the immenſe diſtance of CHINA, together with the monopolies of our INDIA companies, obſtructing the communication, preſerve in EUROPE the gold and ſilver, eſpecially the latter, in much greater plenty than they are found in that kingdom.—But, notwithſtanding this great obſtruction, the force of the cauſes above mentioned is ſtill evident.—The ſkill and ingenuity of *Europe* in general ſurpaſſes perhaps that of *China*, with regard to manual arts and manufactures; yet are we never able to trade thither without great diſadvantage.—And were it not for the continual recruits, which we receive from *America*, money would ſoon *ſink* in EUROPE, and riſe in CHINA, till it came nearly to *a level* in both places.—Nor can any reaſonable man doubt, but *that induſtrious nation*, were they as near us as Poland or Barbary, would drain us of the overplus of our

our ſpecie, and draw to themſelves a larger ſhare of the Weſt Indian treaſures.—We need not have recourſe to a phyſical attraction, in order to explain the neceſſity of this operation.—*There is a moral attraction, ariſing from the intereſts and paſſions of men, which is full as potent and infallible.*

How is the balance kept in the provinces of every kingdom among themſelves, but by the force of this principle, which makes it impoſſible *for money to loſe its level*, and either to riſe or ſink beyond the proportion of the labour and commodities which are in each province? Did not long experience make people eaſy on this head, what a fund of gloomy reflections might calculations afford to a melancholy *Yorkſhireman*, while he computed and magnified the ſums drawn to London by taxes, abſentees, commodities, and found on compariſon the oppoſite articles ſo much inferior?—And no doubt, had the *Heptarchy* ſubſiſted in *England*, the legiſlature of each ſtate had been continually alarmed by the fear of a *wrong balance*; and as it is probable that the mutual hatred of theſe ſtates would have been extremely violent on account of their cloſe neighbourhood, they would have *loaded* and *oppreſſed all commerce*, by a *jealous* and *ſuperfluous caution*.—Since the union has removed the

barriers

barriers between *Scotland* and *England*, which of these nations gains from the other by this free commerce?—Or if the former kingdom has received any increase of riches, can it reasonably be accounted for by any thing but the *increase* of its *art* and *industry?*—It was a common apprehension in *England*, before the union, as we learn from L'ABBE DU BOS *, that *Scotland* would soon drain them of their treasure, were an open trade allowed; and on the other side the *Tweed* a contrary apprehension prevailed: with what justice in both, *time has shewn.*

What happens in small portions of mankind, must take place in greater.—The provinces of the Roman empire, no doubt, kept their balance with each other, and with Italy, independent of the legislature: as much as the several counties of Britain, or the several parishes of each county.—And any man who travels over Europe at this day, may see, by the prices of commodities, that money, in spite of the absurd jealousy of princes and states, has brought itself nearly to a level; and that the difference between one kingdom and another is not greater in this respect, than it is often between different

* *Les interets d'* ANGLETERRE *mal-entendus.*

provinces of the ſame kingdom.—*Men naturally flock to capital cities, ſea-ports, and navigable rivers.—There we find more men, more induſtry, more commodities, and conſequently more money; but ſtill the latter difference holds proportion with the former, and the level is preſerved**.

Our jealouſy and our hatred of *France* are without bounds; and the former ſentiment, at leaſt, muſt be acknowledged reaſonable and well-grounded.—Theſe paſſions have occaſioned innumerable barriers and obſtructions upon commerce, where we are accuſed of being commonly the aggreſſors.—But what have we gained by the bargain?—We loſt the French market for our woollen manufactures, and transferred the commerce of wine to Spain and Portugal, where we buy

* It muſt carefully be remarked, that throughout this diſcourſe, wherever Hume ſpeaks of the level of money, he means always its proportional level to the commodities, labour, induſtry, and ſkill, which is in the ſeveral ſtates.—And he aſſerts, that where theſe advantages are double, triple, quadruple, to what they are in the neighbouring ſtates, the money infallibly will alſo be double, triple, quadruple. The only circumſtance that can obſtruct the exactneſs of theſe proportions, is the expence of tranſporting the commodities from one place to another; and this expence is ſometimes unequal.—Thus the corn, cattle, cheeſe, butter, of Derbyſhire, cannot draw the money of London, ſo much as the manufacture of London draw the money of Derbyſhire.—But this objection is only a ſeeming one: for ſo far as the tranſport of commodities is expenſive, ſo far is the communication between the place obſtructed an imperfect.

worſe liquor at a higher price.—*There are few Engliſhmen who would not think their country abſolutely ruined, were French wines ſold in England ſo cheap and in ſuch abundance as to ſupplant, in ſome meaſure, all ale, and home-brewed liquors: but could we lay aſide prejudice, it would not be difficult to prove, that nothing could be more innocent, perhaps advantageous.—Each new acre of vineyard planted in France, in order to ſupply England with wine, would make it requiſite for the French to take the produce of an Engliſh acre, ſown in wheat or barley, in order to ſubſiſt themſelves; and it is evident, that we ſhould thereby get command of the better commodity.*

There are many edicts of the French king, prohibiting the planting of *new vineyards*, and ordering all thoſe which are lately planted to be grubbed up: ſo ſenſible are they, in that country, of the ſuperior value of *corn*, above every other product.

Mareſchal Vauban complains often, and with reaſon, of the abſurd duties which load the entry of thoſe wines of Languedoc, Guienne, and other ſouthern provinces, that are imported into Britanny and Normandy.—He entertained no doubt but theſe latter provinces could preſerve their balance, notwithſtanding the open commerce which he recommends.—And it is evident, that a few leagues more navigation to England would make no difference; or if it did, that it muſt operate alike on the commodities of both kingdoms.

There is indeed one expedient by which it is poſſible to ſink, and another by which we may raiſe, money beyond its natural level in any kingdom; but theſe caſes, when examined, will be found to reſolve into our general theory, and to bring additional authority to it.

I ſcarcely know any method of ſinking money below its level, but thoſe inſtitutions of *banks*, *funds*, and *paper-credit*, which are ſo much practiſed in this kingdom.—Theſe render *paper equivalent to money*, circulate it through the whole ſtate, make it ſupply the place of gold and ſilver, raiſe proportionably the price of labour and commodities, and by that means either baniſh a great part of thoſe precious metals, or prevent their farther increaſe.—What can be more ſhort-ſighted than our reaſonings on this head?—We fancy, becauſe *an individual* would be much richer, were his ſtock of money doubled, that the ſame good effect would follow were the money of *every one* increaſed; not conſidering, *that this would raiſe as much the price of evèry commodity, and reduce every man, in time, to the ſame condition as before.*—IT IS ONLY IN OUR PUBLIC NEGOCIATIONS AND

TRANS-

TRANSACTIONS WITH FOREIGNERS, THAT A GREATER STOCK OF MONEY IS ADVANTAGEOUS; AND AS OUR PAPER IS THERE ABSOLUTELY INSIGNIFICANT, WE FEEL, BY ITS MEANS, ALL THE ILL EFFECTS ARISING FROM A GREAT ABUNDANCE OF MONEY, WITHOUT REAPING ANY OF THE ADVANTAGES.

Suppoſe that there are 12 millions of *paper*, which circulate in the kingdom as money (for we are not to imagine, that all our enormous funds are employed in that ſhape), and ſuppoſe the real caſh of the kingdom to be 18 millions: here is a ſtate which is found by experience to be able to hold a ſtock of 30 millions.—I ſay, if it be able to hold it, it muſt of neceſſity have acquired it in gold and ſilver, had we not *obſtructed the entrance of theſe metals* by *this new invention of paper.*—Whence would it have acquired that ſum? *From all the kingdoms of the world.*—But why? *Becauſe, if you remove theſe* 12 *millions, money in this ſtate is below its level, compared with our neighbours*; *and we muſt immediately draw from all of them, till we be full and ſaturate, ſo to ſpeak, and can hold no more.*—By our PRESENT POLITICS, we are as careful to *ſtuff* the nation with *this fine commodity* of BANK-BILLS and CHEQUER-NOTES, as if we were afraid of being overburthened with the precious metals.

It

It is not to be doubted, but the great plenty of *bullion* in France is, in a great meaſure, owing to the want of *paper-credit*.—The French have no banks: merchants' bills do not there circulate as with us: uſury, or lending on intereſt, is not directly permitted; ſo that many have large ſums in their coffers: *great quantities of plate are uſed in private houſes*; *and all the churches are full of it*.—By this means, *proviſions* and *labour* ſtill remain *cheaper among them*, than in nations that are not *half ſo rich* in gold and ſilver.—*The advantages of this ſituation, in point of trade as well as in great public emergencies, are too evident to be diſputed* *.

The ſame faſhion a few years ago prevailed in Genoa, which ſtill has place in *England* and *Holland*, of uſing ſervices of china-ware inſtead of plate; but the ſenate, foreſeeing the conſequence, prohibited the uſe of that brittle commodity beyond a certain extent; while the uſe of *ſilver-plate* was left unlimited.—And, I ſuppoſe, in their late diſtreſſes, they felt the good effect of this ordinance.—*Our tax on plate* is, perhaps, in this view, ſomewhat unpolitic.

* This has appeared in their late revolution, when the NATIONAL ASSEMBLY ſanctioned the uſe of *aſſignats* for their *internal* commerce; and employed in their *trade to America* and in their *armies* the *precious metals*, as they are called.

Before

Before the introduction of *paper money* into our colonies, they had gold and ſilver ſufficient for their circulation.—Since the introduction of that commodity, the leaſt inconveniency that has followed is the total baniſhment of the precious metals.—And after the abolition of paper, can it be doubted but money will return, while theſe colonies poſſeſs manufactures and commodities, the only thing valuable in commerce, and for *whoſe ſake alone all men deſire money.*

What pity LYCURGUS *did not think of paper credit, when he wanted to baniſh gold and ſilver from* Sparta!—*It would have ſerved his purpoſe better than the lumps of iron he made uſe of as money; and would alſo have prevented more effectually all commerce with ſtrangers, as being of ſo much leſs real and intrinſic value.*

It muſt, however, be confeſſed, that, as all theſe queſtions of trade and money are extremely complicated, there are certain lights, in which this ſubject may be placed, ſo as to repreſent the *advantages* of PAPER CREDIT and BANKS to be ſuperior to their *diſadvantages.*—That they baniſh ſpecie and bullion from a ſtate is undoubtedly true; and whoever looks no *farther* than this circumſtance does well to condemn them; but ſpecie and bullion are not of ſo great conſequence as not

to

to admit of a compenſation, and even an overbalance from the increaſe of induſtry and of credit, which may be promoted by the *right uſe* of PAPER-MONEY.—It is well known of what advantage it is to a merchant to be able to diſcount his bills *upon occaſion*; and every thing that *facilitates* this ſpecies of traffic is favourable to the general commerce of a ſtate.

There was an invention of this kind, which was fallen upon ſome years ago by the banks of *Edinburgh*; and which, as it is one of the moſt ingenious ideas that has been executed in commerce, has alſo been thought advantageous to *Scotland*.—*It is there called a* BANK-CREDIT; *and is of this nature.—A man goes to the bank and finds ſurety to the amount, we ſhall ſuppoſe, of five thouſand pounds.—This money, or any part of it, he has the liberty of drawing out whenever he pleaſes, and he pays only the ordinary intereſt for it, while it is in his hands.—He may, when he pleaſes, repay any ſum ſo ſmall as twenty pounds, and the intereſt is diſcounted from the very day of the repayment.—The advantages, reſulting from this contrivance, are manifold.—As a man may find ſurety nearly to the amount of his ſubſtance, and his bank-credit is equivalent to ready money, a merchant does hereby in a manner coin his houſes, his houſehold furniture, the goods*

in

in his warehouſe, the foreign debts due to him, his ſhips at ſea; and can, upon occaſion, employ them in all payments, as if they were the current money of the country.—If a man borrow five thouſand pounds from a private hand, beſides that it is not always to be found when required, he pays intereſt for it, whether he be uſing it or not: his bank-credit coſts him nothing except during the very moment, in which it is of ſervice to him: and this circumſtance is of equal advantage as if he had borrowed money at much lower intereſt.—Merchants, likewiſe, from this invention, acquire a great facility in ſupporting each other's credit, which is a conſiderable ſecurity againſt bankruptcies.—A man, when his own bank-credit is exhauſted, goes to any of his neighbours who is not in the ſame condition; and he gets the money, which he replaces at his convenience.

After this practice had taken place during ſome years at *Edinburgh*, ſeveral companies of merchants at *Glaſgow* carried the matter *farther*.—They aſſociated themſelves into different banks, and iſſued notes ſo low as *ten ſhillings*, which they uſed in all payments for goods, manufactures, tradeſmen's labour of all kinds; and theſe notes, from the *eſtabliſhed credit* of the com-

E panies,

panies, *paſſed as money* in all payments throughout the country.—By this means, a ſtock of five thouſand pounds was able to perform the ſame operations as if it were ten or twenty; and merchants were thereby enabled to trade to a *greater extent*, and to require *leſs profit* in all their tranſactions.—But whatever other advantages reſult from theſe inventions, it muſt ſtill be allowed *that they baniſh the precious metals*; and nothing can be a more evident proof of it, than a compariſon of the paſt and preſent condition of Scotland in that particular.—It was found, upon the recoinage made after the union, that there was near *a million of ſpecie in that country:* but notwithſtanding the great increaſe of riches, commerce, and manufactures of all kinds, it is thought, that, even where there is no extraordinary drain made by England, the current ſpecie will not NOW amount to *a third of that ſum.*

But as our projects of PAPER-CREDIT are almoſt the only expedient, by which we can *ſink* money *below its level*; ſo, in my opinion, the only expedient, by which we can *raiſe* money *above it*, is a practice which we ſhould all exclaim againſt as deſtructive, namely, the gathering of large ſums into a public treaſure, *locking*

them

them up, and abſolutely preventing their circulation.—The fluid, not communicating with the neighbouring element, may, by ſuch an artifice, be raiſed to what height we pleaſe.—To prove this, we need only return to our firſt ſuppoſition, of annihilating the half or any part of our caſh; where we found, that the immediate conſequence of ſuch an event would be the attraction of an equal ſum from all the neighbouring kingdoms.—Nor does there ſeem to be any neceſſary bounds ſet, by the nature of things, to this practice of hoarding.—A ſmall city, like Geneva, continuing this policy for ages, might engroſs nine-tenths of the money of Europe.—There ſeems, indeed, in the nature of man, an invincible obſtacle to that immenſe growth of riches.—A WEAK STATE, *with an enormous treaſure, will ſoon become a prey to ſome of its poorer, but more powerful, neighbours.*—A GREAT STATE *would diſſipate its wealth in dangerous and ill-concerted projects; and probably deſtroy, with it, what is much more valuable, the induſtry, morals, and numbers of its people.*—The fluid, in this caſe, raiſed to too great a height, burſts and deſtroys the veſſel that contains it; and mixing itſelf with the ſurrounding element, ſoon falls to its proper level.

From theſe principles we may learn what judgment

we ought to form of those numberless bars, obstructions, and imposts, which all nations of EUROPE, and *none more* than ENGLAND, have put upon trade; from an exorbitant desire of amassing money, which never will heap up beyond its level, while it circulates; or from an ill-grounded apprehension of losing their specie, which never will sink below it.—Could any thing scatter our riches, it would be such *unpolitic contrivances.*—But this general ill effect, however, results from them, that they deprive *neighbouring* nations of that *free communication* and *exchange* which the AUTHOR OF THE WORLD has *intended*, by *giving them* soils, climates, and geniuses, so *different* from each other.

Our MODERN POLITICS *embrace the only method of* BANISHING *money, the using of paper-credit*; they *reject the only method of* AMASSING *it, the practice of hoarding; and they adopt a hundred contrivances*, which serve to no purpose but to *check industry*, and to *rob ourselves* and *our neighbours* of the *common benefits* of ART *and* NATURE.

All taxes, however, upon foreign commodities, are not to be regarded as prejudicial or useless, but those only which are founded on *the jealousy* above mentioned.—*A tax on* GERMAN *linen encourages home manufactures, and thereby multiplies our people and industry.—A tax on*

BRANDY

BRANDY *increaſes the ſale of rum, and ſupports our ſouthern colonies.*—And as it is neceſſary, that impoſts ſhould be levied, for the ſupport of government, it may be thought more convenient to lay them on foreign commodities, which can eaſily be intercepted at the port, and ſubjected to the impoſt.—We ought, however, always to remember the maxim of Dr. SWIFT, that, in the arithmetic of the cuſtoms, two and two make not four, but often make only one.—It can ſcarcely be doubted, but if the duties on wine were *lowered* to a third, they would yield much more to the government than at preſent: our people might thereby afford to drink commonly a *better* and more *wholeſome liquor*; and no prejudice would enſue to *the balance of trade*, of which we are *ſo jealous*.—The manufacture of ale beyond the agriculture is but inconſiderable, and gives employment to few hands.—The tranſport of wine and corn would not be much inferior.

But are there not frequent inſtances, you will ſay, of ſtates and kingdoms, which were formerly rich and opulent, and are now poor and beggarly?—Has not the money left them, with which they formerly abounded?—I anſwer, If they loſe their *trade*, *induſtry*, and *people*, they cannot expect to keep their gold and ſilver: for these precious metals will hold proportion to the former advantages.—When LISBON and AMSTERDAM got the *East-India trade* from VENICE and GENOA, they also got the profits and money which arose from it.—Where the seat of government is transferred, where expensive armies are maintained at a distance, where great funds are possessed by foreigners; there naturally follows from these causes a diminution of the specie.—But these, we may observe, are violent and forcible methods of carrying away money, and are in time commonly attended with the transport of people and industry.—But where these remain, and the drain is not continued, the money always finds its way back again, by a hundred canals, of which we have no notion or suspicion.—*What immense treasures have been spent, by so many nations, in* FLANDERS, *since the revolution, in the course of three long wars? More money perhaps than the half of what is at present in* EUROPE.—*But what has now become of it?—Is it in the narrow compass of the* AUSTRIAN *provinces?—No, surely: it has most of it returned to the several countries whence it came, and has followed that art and industry, by which at first it was acquired.*

IN SHORT, A GOVERNMENT HAS GREAT REASON TO PRESERVE WITH CARE ITS PEOPLE AND ITS MANUFACTURES.

NUFACTURES.—ITS MONEY, IT MAY SAFELY TRUST TO THE COURSE OF HUMAN AFFAIRS, WITHOUT FEAR OR JEALOUSY—OR IF IT EVER GIVE ATTENTION TO THIS LATTER CIRCUMSTANCE, IT OUGHT ONLY TO BE SO FAR AS IT AFFECTS THE FORMER *.

* Hume.

SECT.

SECT. III.

OF THE JEALOUSY OF TRADE.

HAVING endeavoured to remove *one* ſpecies of *ill-founded jealouſy*, which is ſo prevalent among commercial nations, it may not be amiſs to mention *another*, which ſeems *equally groundleſs*.—Nothing is more uſual, among ſtates which have made ſome advances in commerce, than to look on the progreſs of their neighbours with a ſuſpicious eye, *to conſider all trading ſtates as their rivals, and to ſuppoſe that it is impoſſible for any of them to flouriſh, but at their expence*.—In oppoſition to this narrow and malignant opinion, I will venture to aſſert, *that the increaſe of riches and commerce in any one nation, inſtead of hurting, commonly promotes the riches and commerce of all its neighbours; and that a ſtate can ſcarcely carry its trade and induſtry very far, where all the ſurrounding ſtates are buried in ignorance, ſloth, and barbariſm.*

It is obvious, that the *domeſtic induſtry* of a people cannot be hurt by the *greateſt proſperity* of their neighbours;

bours; and as this branch of commerce is undoubtedly the moſt important in any extenſive kingdom, we are ſo far removed from all reaſon of jealouſy.—But I go farther, and obſerve, that *where an open communication is preſerved among nations*, it is impoſſible but the *domeſtic induſtry* of every one muſt receive an increaſe from the improvements of the others.—Compare the ſituation of GREAT BRITAIN at preſent, with what it was two centuries ago.—All the arts both of agriculture and manufactures were then extremely rude and imperfect.—Every improvement, which we have ſince made, has ariſen from our imitation of foreigners; and we ought ſo far to eſteem it happy, that they had previouſly made advances in arts and ingenuity.—But this intercourſe it ſtill upheld to our great advantage: notwithſtanding the advanced ſtate of our manufactures, we daily adopt, in every art, the inventions and improvements of our neighbours.—The commodity is firſt imported from abroad, to our great diſcontent, while we imagine that it drains us of our money: afterwards, the art itſelf is gradually imported, to our *viſible advantage:* yet we continue ſtill to repine, that our neighbours ſhould poſſeſs any art, induſtry, and invention; forgetting that, had they not firſt inſtructed us, we ſhould have been at preſent barbarians; and did they not ſtill continue their inſtructions, the arts muſt fall into a ſtate of languor, and loſe that emulation and novelty, which contribute ſo much to their advancement.

The increaſe of *domeſtic induſtry* lays the foundation of foreign commerce.—Where a great number of commodities are raiſed and perfected for the home-market, there will always be found ſome which can be exported with advantage.—But if our neighbours have no art or cultivation, they cannot take them; becauſe they will have nothing to give in exchange.—In this reſpect, ſtates are in the ſame condition as individuals.—A ſingle man can ſcarcely be induſtrious, where all his fellow-citizens are idle.—The riches of the ſeveral members of a community contribute to increaſe my riches, whatever profeſſion I may follow.—They conſume the produce of my induſtry, and afford me the produce of theirs in return.

Nor needs any ſtate entertain apprehenſions, that their neighbours will improve to ſuch a degree in every art and manufacture, as to have no demand from them.—*Nature, by giving a diverſity of geniuſes, climates, and ſoils, to different nations, has ſecured their mutual intercourſe and commerce, as long as they all remain induſtrious and civilized.*

lized.—Nay, the more the arts increase in any state, the more will be its demands from its industrious neighbours. —The inhabitants, having become opulent and skilful, desire to have every commodity in the utmost perfection; and as they have plenty of commodities to give in exchange, they make large importations from every foreign country.—The industry of the nations, from whom they import, receives encouragement: their own is also increased, by the sale of the commodities which they give in exchange.

But what if a nation has *any staple commodity*, such as the woollen manufactory is in England?—Must not the interfering of their neighbours in *that manufacture* be a loss to them?—I answer, that, when any commodity is denominated the staple of a kingdom, it is supposed that this kingdom has some peculiar and natural advantages for raising the commodity; and if, notwithstanding these advantages, they lose such a manufactory, they ought to blame their own idleness, or expensive government, not the industry of their neighbours.—It ought also to be considered, that, by the increase of industry among the neighbouring nations, the consumption of every particular species of commodity is also increased; and though foreign manufactures interfere with us in the market,

 the

the demand for our product may ſtill continue, or even increaſe.—And ſhould it diminiſh, ought the conſequence to be eſteemed ſo fatal?—If *the ſpirit of induſtry* be preſerved, it may eaſily be diverted from one branch to another; and the manufacturers of wool, for inſtance, be employed in linen, ſilk, iron, or any other commodities, for which there appears to be a demand.—We need not apprehend, that *all* the *objects of induſtry* will be *exhauſted*, or that our manufacturers, while they remain on an equal footing with thoſe of our neighbours, will be in danger of wanting employment.—The emulation among rival nations ſerves rather to keep induſtry alive in all of them: and any people is happier who poſſeſs a variety of manufactures, than if they enjoyed one ſingle great manufacture, in which they are all employed.—Their ſituation is leſs precarious; and they will feel leſs ſenſibly thoſe revolutions and uncertainties, to which every particular branch of commerce will always be expoſed *.

WERE OUR NARROW AND MALIGNANT POLITICS TO MEET WITH SUCCESS, WE SHOULD REDUCE ALL OUR NEIGHBOURING NATIONS TO THE SAME STATE OF SLOTH AND IGNORANCE THAT PREVAILS IN MOROCCO

* HUME.

ROCCO AND THE COAST OF BARBARY.—BUT WHAT WOULD BE THE CONSEQUENCE?—THEY COULD SEND US NO COMMODITIES: THEY COULD TAKE NONE FROM US: OUR DOMESTIC COMMERCE ITSELF WOULD LANGUISH FOR WANT OF EMULATION, EXAMPLE, AND INSTRUCTION: AND WE OURSELVES SHOULD SOON FALL INTO THE SAME ABJECT CONDITION, TO WHICH WE HAD REDUCED THEM.—I SHALL THEREFORE VENTURE TO ACKNOWLEDGE THAT, NOT ONLY AS A MAN, BUT AS A BRITISH SUBJECT, I PRAY FOR THE FLOURISHING COMMERCE OF GERMANY, SPAIN, ITALY, AND EVEN FRANCE ITSELF.—I AM AT LEAST CERTAIN, THAT GREAT BRITAIN, AND ALL THOSE NATIONS, WOULD FLOURISH MORE, DID THEIR SOVEREIGNS AND MINISTERS ADOPT SUCH ENLARGED AND BENEVOLENT SENTIMENTS TOWARDS EACH OTHER.

SECT. IV.

OF PUBLIC CREDIT.

IT appears to have been the common practice of antiquity, to make provision, during peace, for the necessities of war, and to hoard up treasures before-hand, as the instruments either of conquest or defence; without trusting to extraordinary impositions, much less to borrowing, in times of disorder and confusion.—Besides the immense sums above mentioned *, which were amassed by ATHENS, and by the PTOLEMIES, and other successors of Alexander; we learn from Plato †, that the frugal *Lacedemonians* had also collected a great treasure and Arrian ‡ and Plutarch || take notice of the riches which ALEXANDER got possession of on the conquest of *Susa* and *Ecbatana*, and which were reserved, some of them, from the time of Cyrus.—If I remember right, the

* Sect. III. † ALCIB. I. ‡ Lib. iii.

|| PLUT. *in vita* ALEX. He makes these treasures amount to 80,000 talents, or about 15 millions sterling. QUINTUS CURTIUS (lib. v. cap. 2.) says, that Alexander found in Susa above 50,000 talents.

the ſcripture alſo mentions the treaſure of HEZEKIAH and the Jewiſh princes; as profane hiſtory does tha tof PHILIP and PERSEUS, kings of *Macedon.*—The ancient republics of *Gaul* had commonly large ſums in reſerve* Every one knows the treaſure ſeized in *Rome* by JULIUS CÆSAR, during the civil wars; and we find afterwards, that the wiſer emperors, AUGUSTUS, TIBERIUS, VESPASIAN, SEVERUS, &c *always diſcovered the prudent foreſight, of ſaving great ſums againſt any public exigency.*

On the contrary, our MODERN EXPEDIENT, *which has become very general, is to mortgage the public revenues, and to truſt that poſterity will pay off the incumbrances contracted by their anceſtors: and they, having before their eyes ſo good an example of their wiſe fathers, have the ſame prudent reliance on their poſterity; who, at laſt, from neceſſity more than choice, are obliged to place the ſame confidence in a new poſterity.*—But not to waſte time in declaiming againſt a practice which appears ruinous, beyond all controverſy; it ſeems pretty apparent, that the ANCIENT MAXIMS are, in this reſpect, more prudent than the MODERN; even *though the latter had been confined within ſome reaſonable bounds, and had ever, in any inſtance, been attended with*

* STRABO, lib. iv.

ſuch

ſuch frugality, in time of peace, as to diſcharge the debts incurred by an expenſive war.—To truſt to chances and temporary expedients, is, indeed, what the neceſſity of human affairs frequently renders unavoidable; but whoever voluntarily depend on ſuch reſources, have not neceſſity, but their own folly, to accuſe for their misfortunes, when any ſuch befall them.

If the abuſes of treaſures be dangerous, either by engaging the ſtate in raſh enterprizes, or making it neglect military diſcipline, in confidence of its riches; the abuſes of mortgaging are more certain and inevitable; poverty, impotence, and ſubjection to foreign powers

According to MODERN POLICY *war is attended with every deſtructive circumſtance; loſs of men, increaſe of taxes, decay of commerce, diſſipation of money, devaſtation by ſea and land.*—According to ANCIENT MAXIMS, the opening of the public treaſure, as it produced an uncommon affluence of gold and ſilver, ſerved as a temporary encouragement to induſtry, and atoned, in *ſome degree*, for the *inevitable calamities* of war.

IT IS VERY TEMPTING TO A MINISTER TO EMPLOY SUCH AN EXPEDIENT, AS ENABLES HIM TO MAKE A GREAT FIGURE DURING HIS ADMINISTRATION, WITHOUT OVERBURTHENING THE PEOPLE WITH

TAXES, OR EXCITING ANY IMMEDIATE CLAMOURS AGAINST HIMSELF.—THE PRACTICE, THEREFORE, OF CONTRACTING DEBT WILL ALMOST INFALLIBLY BE ABUSED, IN EVERY GOVERNMENT.—IT WOULD SCARCELY BE MORE IMPRUDENT TO GIVE A PRODIGAL SON A CREDIT IN EVERY BANKER'S SHOP IN LONDON, THAN TO IMPOWER A STATESMAN TO DRAW BILLS, IN THIS MANNER, UPON POSTERITY.

What then ſhall we ſay to the NEW PARADOX, that *public incumbrances* are, of themſelves, *advantageous*, independent of the neceſſity of contracting them; and that any ſtate, even though it were not preſſed by a foreign enemy, could not poſſibly have embraced a *wiſer expedient* for *promoting commerce* and *riches*, than to *create funds*, and *debts*, and *taxes*, *without limitation?*—Reaſonings, ſuch as theſe, might naturally have paſſed for trials of wit among rhetoricians, like the panegyrics on folly and a fever, on BUSIRIS and NERO, had we not ſeen *ſuch abſurd maxims patronized by great miniſters*, and by *a whole party* among us.

Let us examine the conſequences of public debts, both in our *domeſtic* management, by their influence on commerce and induſtry; and in our *foreign* tranſactions, by their effect on wars and negociations.

First, It is certain, that national debts *cause a mighty confluence of people and riches to the capital*, by the great sums, levied in the provinces to pay the interest; and perhaps, too, by the advantages in trade above mentioned, which they give the merchants in the capital above the rest of the kingdom.—The question is, whether, in our case, it be for the public interest, that so many privileges should be conferred on London, which has already arrived at such an enormous size, and seems still increasing?—Some men are apprehensive of the consequences.—For my own part, I cannot forbear thinking, that, though the head is undoubtedly too large for the body, yet that great city is so happily situated, that its excessive bulk causes less inconvenience than even a smaller capital to a greater kingdom.—There is more difference between the prices of all provisions in Paris and Languedoc, than between those in London and Yorkshire.—*The immense greatness, indeed, of* London, *under a government which admits not of discretionary power, renders the people factious, mutinous, seditious, and even perhaps rebellious.*—But to this evil the *national debts* themselves tend to provide a remedy.—The first visible eruption, or even immediate danger, of public disorders, must alarm all the stock-holders, whose property is the moſt precarious of any; and will make them fly to the ſupport of government, whether menaced by Jacobitiſh violence or democratical frenzy.

Secondly, Public ſtocks, being a kind of paper-credit, have all the diſadvantages attending that ſpecies of money. —*They baniſh gold and ſilver from the moſt conſiderable commerce of the ſtate, reduce them to common circulation, and by that means render all proviſions and labour dearer than otherwiſe they would be.*

Thirdly, The taxes, which are levied to pay the intereſts of theſe debts, are apt either to *heighten the price of labour*, or be *an oppreſſion on the poorer ſort.*

Fourthly, As foreigners poſſeſs a great ſhare of our national funds, they render the public, in a manner, tributary to them, and may in time occaſion the tranſport of our people and our induſtry.

Fifthly, The greateſt part of public ſtock being always in the hands of *idle people*, who live on their revenue, our funds give great encouragement to an *uſeleſs, gambling*, and *unactive life.*

But though the injury that ariſes to commerce and induſtry from our public funds, will appear, upon balancing the whole, not inconſiderable, it is trivial, in compariſon of the prejudice that reſults to the ſtate conſidered as a body politic, which muſt ſupport itſelf in the ſociety of nations, and have various tranſactions with other ſtates.—The ill, there, is pure and unmixed, without any favourable circumſtance to atone for it; and it is an ill too of a nature the higheſt and moſt important.

We have, indeed, been *told*, that the public is no weaker upon account of its debts; ſince they are moſtly due among ourſelves, and bring as much property to one as they take from another.—*It is like transferring money from the right hand to the left; which leaves the perſon neither richer nor poorer than before.*—Such looſe reaſonings and ſpecious compariſons will always paſs, where we judge not upon principles.—I aſk, Is it poſſible, in the nature of things, to overburthen a nation with taxes, even where the ſovereign reſides among them?—*The very doubt ſeems extravagant*; ſince it is requiſite, in every community, that there be a certain proportion obſerved between the laborious and the idle part of it.—*But if all our preſent taxes be mortgaged, muſt we not invent new ones? And may not this matter be carried to a length that is ruinous and deſtructive?*

In every nation, there are always ſome methods of levying money more eaſy than others, agreeably to the

way

way of living of the people, and the commodities they make ufe of.—In Britain, the excifes upon malt and beer afford a large revenue; becaufe the operations of malting and brewing are tedious, and are impoffible to be concealed; and at the fame time, thefe commodities are not fo abfolutely neceffary to life, as that the raifing their price would very much affect the poorer fort.—*Thefe taxes being all mortgaged, what difficulty to find new ones! what vexation and ruin of the poor!*

It will fcarcely be afferted, that no bounds ought ever to be fet to national debts; and that the public would be no weaker, were twelve or fifteen fhillings in the pound, land-tax, mortgaged, with all the prefent cuftoms and excifes.—There is fomething, therefore, in the cafe, befide the mere transferring of property from one hand to another.

Suppofe the public once fairly brought to that condition, to which it is haftening with fuch amazing rapidity; fuppofe the land to be taxed eighteen or nineteen fhillings in the pound; for it can never bear the whole twenty; fuppofe all the excifes and cuftoms to be fcrewed up to the utmoft which the nation can bear, without entirely lofing its commerce and induftry; and fuppofe that all thofe funds are mortgaged to perpetuity, and that the invention and wit of all our projectors can find no new imposition, which may serve as the foundation of a new loan; and let us consider the necessary consequences of this situation.—Though the imperfect state of our political knowledge, and the narrow capacities of men, make it difficult to foretel the effects which will result from any untried measure, the seeds of ruin are here scattered with such profusion as not to escape the eye of the most careless observer.

Though a resolution should be formed by the legislature never to impose any tax which hurts commerce and discourages industry, it will be impossible for men, in subjects of *such extreme delicacy*, to reason so justly as never to be mistaken, or, amidst *difficulties so urgent*, never to be seduced from their resolution.—The continual fluctuations in commerce require continual alterations in the nature of the taxes; which exposes the legislature every moment to the danger both of wilful and involuntary error.—And any great blow given to trade, whether by injudicious taxes or by other accidents, throws the whole system of government into confusion.

I must confess, that there is a strange supineness, from long custom, creeped into all ranks of men, with regard to public debts, not unlike what divines so vehemently complain of with regard to their religious doctrines.—

We

We all own, that the moſt ſanguine imagination cannot hope, either that this or any future miniſtry will be poſſeſſed of ſuch rigid and ſteady frugality, as to make a conſiderable progreſs in the payment of our debts; or that the ſituation of foreign affairs will, for any long time, allow them leiſure and tranquillity for ſuch an undertaking.—*What then is to become of us?*—Were we ever ſo good Chriſtians, and ever ſo reſigned to Providence; this, methinks, were a curious queſtion, even conſidered as a ſpeculative one, and what it might not be altogether impoſſible to form ſome conjectural ſolution of.—The events here will depend little upon the contingencies of battles, negociations, intrigues, and factions.—There ſeems to be a natural progreſs of things, which may guide our reaſoning.—As it would have required but a moderate ſhare of prudence, when we firſt began this practice of mortgaging, to have foretold, from the nature of men and of miniſters, that things would neceſſarily be carried to the length we ſee; ſo now, that they have at laſt happily reached it, it may not be difficult to gueſs at the conſequences.—IT MUST, INDEED, BE ONE OF THESE TWO EVENTS; EITHER THE NATION MUST DESTROY PUBLIC CREDIT, OR PUBLIC CREDIT WILL DESTROY THE NATION.—It

is

is impoſſible that they can both ſubſiſt, after the manner they have been hitherto managed, in this, as well as in ſome other countries.—*But it is more probable, that the breach of national faith will be the neceſſary effect of wars, defeats, misfortunes, and public calamities, or even perhaps of victories and conqueſts.*—I MUST CONFESS, WHEN SEE PRINCES AND STATES FIGHTING AND QUARRELLING, AMIDST THEIR DEBTS, FUNDS, AND PUBLIC MORTGAGES, IT ALWAYS BRINGS TO MY MIND A MATCH OF CUDGEL-PLAYING FOUGHT IN A CHINA SHOP!!

How can it be expected, that ſovereigns will ſpare a ſpecies of property, which is pernicious to themſelves and to the public, when they have ſo little compaſſion on lives and properties, that are uſeful to both?—Let the time come (and ſurely it will come) when the *new funds*, created for the exigencies of the year, are not ſubſcribed to, and raiſe not the money projected.—Suppoſe, either that the caſh of the nation is exhauſted; or that our faith, which has been hitherto ſo ample, begins to fail us.—Suppoſe that, in this diſtreſs, the nation is threatened with an invaſion; a rebellion is ſuſpected or broken out at home; a ſquadron cannot be equipped for want of pay, victuals, or repairs; or even a foreign ſubſidy

subsidy cannot be advanced.—What must a prince or minister do in such an emergency?—The right of self-preservation is unalienable in every individual, much more in every community.—And the folly of our statesmen must then be greater than the folly of those who first contracted debt, or, what is more, than that of those who trusted, or continue to trust, this security, if these statesmen have the means of safety in their hands, and do not employ them.—The funds, created and mortgaged, will, by that time, bring in a large yearly revenue, sufficient for the defence and security of the nation: money is perhaps lying in the exchequer, ready for the discharge of the quarterly interest: *Necessity calls, fear urges, reason exhorts, compassion alone exclaims: the money will immediately be seized for the current service, under the most solemn protestations, perhaps, of being immediately replaced.*—But no more is requisite.—*The whole fabric, already tottering, falls to the ground, and buries thousands in its ruins.*—And this, I think, may be called the NATURAL DEATH of public credit: for to this period it tends as *naturally* as an animal body to its dissolution and destruction.

So great dupes are the generality of mankind, that, notwithstanding such a violent shock to public credit, as a voluntary bankruptcy in England would occaſion, it would not probably be long, ere credit would again revive in as flouriſhing a condition as before.—The late king of France, during the laſt war, borrowed money at lower intereſt than ever his grandfather did; and as low as the Britiſh parliament, comparing the natural rate of intereſt in both kingdoms.—And though men are commonly more governed by what they have ſeen, than by what they foreſee, with whatever certainty; yet promiſes, proteſtations, fair appearances, with the allurements of preſent intereſt, have ſuch powerful influence as few are able to reſiſt.—Mankind are, in all ages, caught by the ſame baits: the ſame tricks, played over and over again, ſtill trepan them.—The heights of popularity and patriotiſm are ſtill the beaten road to power and tyranny; flattery to treachery; ſtanding armies to arbitrary government; and the glory of God to the temporal intereſt of the clergy.—The fear of an everlaſting deſtruction of credit, allowing it to be an evil, is a needleſs bugbear.—A prudent man, in reality, would rather lend to the public immediately after they had taken a ſpunge to their debts, than at preſent; as much as an opulent knave, even though one could not force him to pay, is a preferable debtor to an honeſt bankrupt:

bankrupt: for the former, in order to carry on bufinefs, may find it his intereft to difcharge his debts, where they are not exorbitant; the latter has it not in his power.—The reafoning of Tacitus *, as it is eternally true, is very applicable to our prefent cafe.—Sed vulgus ad magnitudinem beneficiorum aderat: ftultiffimus quifque pecuniis mercabatur: Apud fapientes caffa habebantur, quæ neque dari neque accipi, falva republica, poterant. *The public is a debtor, whom no man can oblige to pay.—The only check which the creditors have upon her, is the intereft of preferving credit; an intereft, which may eafily be overbalanced by a great debt, and by a difficult and extraordinary emergence, even fuppofing that credit irrecoverable.*—Not to mention, that a prefent neceffity often forces ftates into meafures, which are, ftrictly fpeaking, againft their intereft.

Thefe two events, fuppofed above, are calamitous, but not the moft calamitous—Thoufands are thereby facrificed to the fafety of millions.—But we are not without danger, that the contrary event may take place, and that millions may be facrificed for ever to the temporary fafety of thoufands.—Our popular government, perhaps, will render it difficult or dangerous for a minifter to ven-

* Hift. lib. iii.

ture on ſo deſperate an expedient, as that of a *voluntary bankruptcy.*—And though the Houſe of Lords be altogether compoſed of proprietors of land, and the Houſe of Commons chiefly; and conſequently neither of them can be ſuppoſed to have great property in the funds: yet the connections of the members may be ſo great with the proprietors, as to render them more tenacious of public faith, than prudence, policy, or even juſtice, ſtrictly ſpeaking, requires.—And perhaps too, our foreign enemies may be ſo politic as to diſcover, that our ſafety lies in deſpair, and may not, therefore, ſhow the danger, open and barefaced, till it be inevitable.—*The balance of power in* EUROPE, *our grandfathers, our fathers, and we, have all eſteemed too unequal to be preſerved without our attention and aſſiſtance.—But our children, weary of the ſtruggle, and fettered with incumbrances, may ſit down ſecure, and ſee their neighbours oppreſſed and conquered; till, at laſt, they themſelves and their creditors lie both at the mercy of the conqueror.*—And this may properly enough be denominated the VIOLENT DEATH of our public credit*.

THESE SEEM TO BE THE EVENTS, WHICH ARE NOT VERY REMOTE, AND WHICH REASON FORESEES AS

* HUME.

CLEARLY

CLEARLY ALMOST AS SHE CAN DO ANY THING THAT LIES IN THE WOMB OF TIME.—AND THOUGH THE ANCIENTS MAINTAINED, THAT IN ORDER TO REACH THE GIFT OF PROPHECY, A CERTAIN DIVINE FURY OR MADNESS WAS REQUISITE, ONE MAY SAFELY AFFIRM, THAT, IN ORDER TO DELIVER SUCH PROPHECIES AS THESE, NO MORE IS NECESSARY, THAN MERELY TO BE IN ONE'S SENSES, FREE FROM THE INFLUENCE OF POPULAR MADNESS AND DELUSION.

SECT. V.

OF PUBLIC DEBTS.

In that rude ſtate of ſociety which precedes the extenſion of commerce and the improvement of manufactures, when thoſe expenſive luxuries which commerce and manufactures can alone introduce are altogether unknown, the perſon who poſſeſſes a large revenue, can ſpend or enjoy that revenue in no other way than by maintaining nearly as many people as it can maintain.—An *hoſpitality* in which there is *no luxury*, and a liberality in which there is *no oſtentation*, occaſion, in this ſituation of things, the principal expences of the rich and the great.—But theſe are expences by which people are not very apt to ruin themſelves.—There is not, perhaps, any ſelfiſh pleaſure ſo frivolous, of which the purſuit has not ſometimes ruined even ſenſible men.—A paſſion for cock-fighting has ruined many.—But the inſtances, I believe, are not very numerous of people who have been ruined by a hoſpitality or liberality of this kind; though the hoſpitality of luxury and the liberality of ostentation have ruined many. Among our feudal anceſtors, the long time during which eſtates uſed to continue in the ſame family, ſufficiently demonſtrates the general diſpoſition of people to live within their income.

In a commercial country abounding with every ſort of expenſive luxury, the ſovereign, in the ſame manner as almoſt all the great proprietors in his dominions, naturally ſpends a great part of his revenue in purchaſing luxuries.—His own and the neighbouring countries ſupply him abundantly with all the coſtly trinkets which compoſe the ſplendid, but inſignificant, pageantry of a court.—His ordinary expence becomes equal to his ordinary revenue, and it is well if it does not frequently exceed it.—The amaſſing of treaſure can no longer be expected, and when extraordinary exigencies require extraordinary expences, he muſt neceſſarily call upon his ſubjects for an extraordinary aid.—The late King of Pruſſia and his father are the only great princes of Europe, who, ſince the death of Henry IV. of France in 1610, are ſuppoſed to have amaſſed any conſiderable treaſure.—The parſimony which leads to accumulation has become almoſt as rare in *republican* as in monarchical governments.—The Italian republics, the United Pro-

vinces

vinces of the Netherlands, are all in debt.—The canton of Berne is the ſingle republic in Europe which has amaſſed any conſiderable treaſure. — The other Swiſs republics have not.—The taſte for ſome ſort of pageantry, for ſplendid buildings, at leaſt, and other public ornaments, frequently prevails as much in the apparently ſober ſenate-houſe of a little republic, as in the diſſipated court of the greateſt king.

The want of parſimony in time of peace, impoſes the neceſſity of contracting debt in time of war.—When war comes, there is no money in the treaſury but what is neceſſary for carrying on the ordinary expence of the peace eſtabliſhment.—In war an eſtabliſhment of three or four times that expence becomes neceſſary for the defence of the ſtate, and conſequently a revenue three or four times greater than the peace revenue.—Suppoſing that the ſovereign ſhould have, what he ſcarce ever has, the immediate means of augmenting his revenue in proportion to the augmentation of his expence, yet ſtill the produce of the taxes, from which this increaſe of revenue muſt be drawn, will not begin to come into the treaſury till perhaps ten or twelve months after they are impoſed. —But the moment in which war begins, or rather the moment in which it appears likely to begin, the army

muſt

muſt be augmented, the fleet muſt be fitted out, the garriſoned towns muſt be put into a poſture of defence; that army, that fleet, thoſe garriſoned towns, muſt be furniſhed with arms, ammunition, and proviſions.—An immediate and great expence muſt be incurred in that moment of immediate danger, which will not wait for the gradual and ſlow returns of the new taxes.—In this exigency government can have no other reſource but in *borrowing*.

A country abounding with merchants and manufacturers, neceſſarily abounds with a ſet of people through whoſe hands not only their own capitals, but the capitals of all thoſe who either lend them money, or truſt them with goods, paſs as frequently, or more frequently, than the revenue of a private man, who, without trade or buſineſs, lives upon his income, paſſes through his hands. —The revenue of ſuch a man can regularly paſs through his hands only once in a year.—But the whole amount of the capital and credit of a merchant, who deals in a trade of which the returns are very quick, may ſometimes paſs through his hands two, three, or four times, in a year.—A country abounding with merchants and manufacturers, therefore, neceſſarily abounds with a ſet of people who have it at all times in their power to advance, if they choose to do so, a very large sum of money to government.—*Hence the ability in the subjects of a commercial state to lend.*

Commerce and manufactures can seldom flourish long in any state which does not enjoy a regular administration of justice, in which the people do not feel themselves secure in the possession of their property, in which the faith of contracts is not supported by law, and in which the authority of the state is not supposed to be regularly employed in enforcing the payment of debts from all those who are able to pay.—Commerce and manufactures, in short, can seldom flourish in any state in which there is not a certain degree of confidence in the justice of government.—The same confidence which disposes great merchants and manufacturers, upon ordinary occasions, to trust their property to the protection of a particular government, disposes them, upon extraordinary occasions, to trust that government with the use of their property.—By lending money to government, they do not even for a moment diminish their ability to carry on their trade and manufactures.—On the contrary, they commonly augment it.—The necessities of the state render government upon most occasions willing to borrow upon terms extremely advantageous to the lender.—The ſecurity which it grants to the original creditor, is made transferable to any other creditor, and, from the univerſal confidence in the juſtice of the ſtate, generally ſells in the market for more than was originally paid for it.—The merchant or monied man makes money by lending money to government, and inſtead of diminiſhing, increaſes his trading capital.—He generally conſiders it as a favour, therefore, when the adminiſtration admits him to a ſhare in the firſt ſubſcription for a new loan.—*Hence the inclination or willingneſs in the ſubjects of a commercial ſtate to lend.*

THE GOVERNMENT OF SUCH A STATE IS VERY APT TO REPOSE ITSELF UPON THIS ABILITY AND WILLINGNESS OF ITS SUBJECTS TO LEND THEIR MONEY ON EXTRAORDINARY OCCASIONS.—IT FORESEES THE FACILITY OF BORROWING, AND THEREFORE DISPENSES ITSELF FROM THE DUTY OF SAVING.

In a rude ſtate of ſociety there are no great mercantile or manufacturing capitals.—The individuals, who hoard whatever money they can ſave, and who conceal their hoard, do ſo from a diſtruſt of the juſtice of government, from a fear that if it was known that they had a hoard, and where that hoard was to be found, they would quickly be plundered.—In ſuch a ſtate of things few people would be able, and nobody would be willing, to lend their money to government on extraordinary exigencies.—The sovereign feels that he must provide for such exigencies by saving, because he foresees the absolute impossibility of borrowing.—This foresight increases still further his natural disposition to save.

THE PROGRESS OF THE ENORMOUS DEBTS WHICH AT PRESENT OPPRESS, AND WILL IN THE LONG-RUN PROBABLY RUIN, ALL THE GREAT NATIONS OF EUROPE, HAS BEEN PRETTY UNIFORM.—Nations, like private men, have generally begun to borrow upon what may be called personal credit, without assigning or mortgaging any particular fund for the payment of the debt; and when this resource has failed them, they have gone on to borrow upon assignments or mortgages of particular funds.

In Great Britain the annual land and malt taxes are regularly anticipated every year, by virtue of a borrowing clause constantly inserted into the acts which impose them.—The bank of England generally advances at an interest, which since the revolution has varied from eight to three *per cent.* the sums for which those taxes are granted, and receives payment as their produce gradually comes in.—If there is a deficiency, which there

always

always is, it is provided for in the ſupplies of the enſuing year.—The only conſiderable branch of the public revenue which yet remains unmortgaged is thus regularly ſpent before it comes in.—*Like an improvident ſpendthrift, whoſe preſſing occaſions will not allow him to wait for the regular payment of his revenue, the ſtate is in the conſtant practice of borrowing of its own factors and agents, and of paying intereſt for the uſe of its own money.*

In the reign of King WILLIAM, and during a great part of that of Queen ANNE, before we had become ſo familiar as we are now with the practice of perpetual funding, the greater part of the new taxes were impoſed but for a ſhort period of time (for four, five, ſix, or ſeven years only), and a great part of the grants of every year conſiſted in loans upon *anticipations* of the produce of thoſe taxes.—The produce being frequently inſufficient for paying within the limited term the principal and intereſt of the money borrowed, deficiencies aroſe, to make good which it became neceſſary to prolong the term.

In conſequence of different ſubſequent acts, the greater part of the taxes which before had been anticipated only for a ſhort term of years, were rendered *perpetual* as a fund

fund for paying, *not the capital*, but *the intereſt only*, of the money which had been borrowed upon them by different ſucceſſive anticipations.

Had money never been raiſed but by anticipation, the courſe of a few years would have liberated the public revenue, without any other attention of government beſides that of not overloading the fund by charging it with more debt than it could pay within the limited term, and of not anticipating a ſecond time before the expiration of the firſt anticipation.—*But the greater part of European governments have been incapable of thoſe attentions.*—They have frequently overloaded the fund even upon the firſt anticipation; and when this happened not to be the caſe, they have generally taken care to overload it, by anticipating a ſecond and a third time before the expiration of the firſt anticipation.—The fund becoming in this manner altogether inſufficient for paying both principal and intereſt of the money borrowed upon it, it became neceſſary to charge it with the *intereſt* only, or a perpetual annuity equal to the intereſt, and ſuch unprovident *anticipations* neceſſarily gave birth to the more ruinous practice of *perpetual funding*.—But though this practice neceſſarily puts off the liberation of the public revenue from a fixed period to one ſo indefinite

finite THAT IT IS NOT VERY LIKELY EVER TO ARRIVE; yet as a greater ſum can in all caſes be raiſed by this new practice than by the old one of anticipations, the former, when men have once become familiar with it, has in the great exigencies of the ſtate been univerſally preferred to the latter.—*To relieve the preſent exigency is always the object which principally intereſts thoſe immediately concerned in the adminiſtration of public affairs.—The future liberation of the public revenue, they leave to the care of poſterity.*

Beſides thoſe two methods of borrowing, by anticipations and by perpetual funding, there are two other methods, which hold a ſort of middle place between them.—Theſe are, that of borrowing upon annuities for terms of years, and that of borrowing upon annuities for lives.

In England, the ſeat of government being in the greateſt mercantile city in the world, the merchants are generally the people who advance money to government.—By advancing it they do not mean to diminiſh, but, on the contrary, to increaſe their mercantile capitals; and unleſs they expected to ſell with ſome profit their ſhare in the ſubſcription for a new loan, they never would ſubſcribe.

The

The ordinary expence of the greater part of modern governments in time of peace being equal or nearly equal to their ordinary revenue, when WAR *comes*, they are both *unwilling* and *unable* to increaſe their revenue in proportion to the increaſe of their expence.—*They are* UNWILLING, *for fear of offending the people, who by ſo great and ſo ſudden an increaſe of taxes, would ſoon be diſguſted with the war; and they are* UNABLE, *from not well knowing what taxes would be ſufficient to produce the revenue wanted.*—The facility of *borrowing* delivers them from the embarraſſment which this fear and inability would otherwiſe occaſion.—By means of *borrowing* they are enabled, with a very moderate increaſe of taxes, to raiſe, from year to year, money ſufficient for carrying on the war, and by the practice of perpetual funding they are enabled, with the ſmalleſt poſſible increaſe of taxes, to raiſe annually the largeſt poſſible ſum of money.

The return of peace, indeed, ſeldom relieves the nation from the greater part of the taxes impoſed during war.—Theſe are mortgaged for *the intereſt* of the debt contracted in order to carry it on.—If, over and above paying the intereſt of this debt, and defraying the ordinary expence of government, the old revenue, together

with

with the new taxes, produce ſome ſurplus revenue, it may *perhaps* be converted into a *ſinking fund* for paying off the debt.—But, in the firſt place, this ſinking fund, even ſuppoſing it ſhould be applied to no other purpoſe, is generally altogether inadequate for paying, in the courſe of any period during which it can reaſonably be expected that peace ſhould continue, the whole debt contracted during the war; and, in the ſecond place, this fund is almoſt always applied to other purpoſes.

The new taxes were impoſed for the ſole purpoſe of paying the intereſt of the money borrowed upon them. —If they produce more, it is generally ſomething which was neither intended nor expected, and is therefore ſeldom very conſiderable.

During the moſt profound peace, various events occur which require an extraordinary expence, and government finds it always more convenient to defray this expence by *miſapplying* the *ſinking fund* than by impoſing a *new tax*.—Every new tax is immediately felt more or leſs by the people.—It occaſions always ſome murmur, and meets with ſome oppoſition.—The more taxes may have been multiplied, the higher they may have been raiſed upon every different ſubject of taxation; the more loudly the people complain of every new tax, the more difficult it becomes too either to find out new ſubjects of taxation, or to raiſe much higher the taxes already impoſed upon the old.—A momentary ſuſpenſion of the payment of debt is not immediately felt by the people, and occaſions neither murmur nor complaint.—*To borrow of the ſinking fund is always an obvious and eaſy expedient for getting out of the preſent difficulty.*—The more the public debts may have been accumulated, the more neceſſary it may have become to ſtudy to reduce them, the more dangerous, the more ruinous it may be to miſapply any part of the ſinking fund; the leſs likely is the public debt to be reduced to any conſiderable degree, the more likely, the more certainly is the ſinking fund to be miſapplied towards defraying all the extraordinary expences which occur in time of peace.—When a nation is already overburdened with taxes, nothing but the neceſſities of a new war, nothing but either the animoſity of national vengeance, or the anxiety for national ſecurity, can induce the people to ſubmit, with tolerable patience, to a new tax.—*Hence the uſual miſapplication of the ſinking fund.*

Were the expence of war to be defrayed always by a revenue raiſed within the year, the taxes from which that extraordinary revenue was drawn would laſt no

longer

longer than the war.—The ability of private people to accumulate, though lefs during the war, would have been greater during the peace than under the fyftem of funding.—War would not neceffarily have occafioned the deftruction of any old capitals, and peace would have occafioned the accumulation of many more new.—*Wars* would in general be *more fpeedily concluded*, and *lefs wantonly undertaken*.—The people feeling, during the continuance of war, the complete burden of it, would foon grow weary of it, and government, in order to humour them, would not be under the neceffity of carrying it on longer than it was neceffary to do fo.—The forefight of the heavy and unavoidable burdens of war would hinder the people from wantonly calling for it, when there was no real or folid intereft to fight for.

When funding, befides, has made a certain progrefs, the multiplication of taxes which it brings along with it fometimes impairs as much the ability of private people to accumulate even in time of peace, as the other fyftem would in time of war.—The peace revenue of Great Britain amounts at prefent to more than ten millions a year.—If free and unmortgaged, it might be fufficient, with proper management, and without contracting a fhilling of new debt, to carry on the moft vigorous war.

—The

—The private revenue of the inhabitants of Great Britain is at prefent as much encumbered in time of peace, their ability to accumulate it as much impaired as it would have been in the time of the moft expenfive war, had the pernicious fyftem of funding never been adopted.

In the payment of the intereft of the public debt, it has been faid, " it is the right hand which pays the left. " The money does not go out of the country. It is " only a part of the revenue of one fet of the inhabitants " which is transferred to another; and the nation is not " a farthing the poorer."—*This apology* is founded altogether in the *fophiftry* of the *mercantile fyftem**.—It fuppofes, befides, that the whole public debt is owing to the inhabitants of the country, which happens not to be true; the Dutch, as well as feveral other foreign nations, having a very confiderable fhare in our public funds.—But though the whole debt were owing to the inhabitants of the country, it would not upon that account be *lefs pernicious*.

LAND and CAPITAL STOCK are the two original

* This is proved a little further on. " To TRANSFER *from—to*, &c." which fee page 78.

fources

ſources of all revenue both private and public.—Capital ſtock pays the wages of productive labour, whether employed in agriculture, manufactures, or commerce.—The management of thoſe two original ſources of revenue belongs to two different ſets of people; the proprietors of land, and the owners or employers of capital ſtock.

The proprietor of LAND is intereſted for the ſake of his own revenue to keep his eſtate in as good condition as he can, by building and repairing his tenants houſes, by making and maintaining the neceſſary drains and encloſures, and all thoſe other expenſive improvements which it properly belongs to the landlord to make and maintain.—But by different land-taxes the revenue of the landlord may be ſo much diminiſhed; and by different duties upon the neceſſaries and conveniencies of life, that diminiſhed revenue may be rendered of ſo little real value, that he may find himſelf altogether unable to make or maintain thoſe expenſive improvements.—When the landlord, however, ceaſes to do his part, it is altogether impoſſible that the tenant ſhould continue to do his.—As the diſtreſs of the landlord increaſes, the farm, or town houſe, muſt neceſſarily decline.

When, by different taxes upon the neceſſaries and conveniencies

conveniencies of life, *the owners* and *employers* of CAPITAL STOCK find, that whatever revenue they derive from it, will not, in a particular country, purchase the same quantity of those necessaries and conveniencies which an equal revenue would in almost any other, they will be disposed to remove to some other.—And when, in order to raise those taxes, all or the greater part of merchants and manufacturers, that is, all or the greater part of the employers of great capitals, come to be continually exposed to the mortifying and vexatious visits of the tax-gatherers, this disposition to remove will soon be changed into an actual removal.—The industry of the country will necessarily fall with the removal of the capital which supported it, and the ruin of trade and manufactures will follow the declension of agriculture.

To TRANSFER *from* the owners of those two great sources of revenue, land and capital stock, *from* the persons immediately interested in the good condition of every particular portion of land, and in the good management of every particular portion of capital stock, *to* another set of persons *(the creditors of the public*, who have *no such particular interest)*, the greater part of the revenue arising from either must, in the long-run, occasion

both

both the neglect of land, and the waste or removal of capital stock.—A creditor of the public has no doubt a general interest in the prosperity of the agriculture, manufactures, and commerce of the country; and consequently in the good condition of its lands, and in the good management of its capital stock.—Should there be any general failure or declension in any of these things, the produce of the different taxes might no longer be sufficient to pay him the annuity or interest which is due to him.—But a creditor of the public, considered merely as such, has no interest in the good condition of any particular portion of land, or in the good management of any particular portion of capital stock.—As a creditor of the public he has no knowledge of any such *particular* portion.—He has no inspection of it.—He can have no care about it.—Its ruin may in some cases be unknown to him, and cannot directly affect him.

The practice of funding has gradually enfeebled every state which has adopted it.—The ITALIAN republics seem to have begun it.—GENOA and VENICE, the only two remaining which can pretend to an independent existence, have both been enfeebled by it.—SPAIN seems to have learned the practice from the Italian republics, and (its taxes being probably leſs judicious than theirs) it has, in proportion to its natural ſtrength, been ſtill more enfeebled.—The debts of Spain are of very old ſtanding.—It was deeply in debt before the end of the ſixteenth century, about a hundred years before England owed a ſhilling.—FRANCE, notwithſtanding all its natural reſources, languiſhed under an oppreſſive load of the ſame kind.—The republic of the UNITED PROVINCES is as much enfeebled by its debts as either Genoa or Venice.—Is it likely that in GREAT BRITAIN alone a practice, which has brought either weakneſs or deſolation into every other country, ſhould prove altogether innocent?

The ſyſtem of taxation eſtabliſhed in thoſe different countries, it may be ſaid, is inferior to that of England. —I believe it is ſo.—But it ought to be remembered, that when the wiſeſt government has exhauſted all the *proper ſubjects of taxation*, it muſt, in caſes of urgent neceſſity, have recourſe to *improper ones*.—The wiſe republic of HOLLAND has upon ſome occaſions been obliged to have recourſe to taxes as inconvenient as the greater part of thoſe of SPAIN.—*Another war begun before any conſiderable liberation of the public revenue had been brought about, and growing in its progreſs as expenſive as the*

the last war, may, from irresistible necessity, render the British system of taxation as oppressive as that of HOLLAND, *or even as that of* SPAIN.—To the honour of our present system of taxation, indeed, it has *hitherto* given so little embarrassment to industry, that, during the course even of the most expensive wars, the frugality and good conduct of individuals seem to have been able, by saving and accumulation, to repair all the breaches which the *waste* and *extravagance* of GOVERNMENT had made in the general capital of the society.—At the conclusion of the late war, the most expensive that GREAT BRITAIN ever waged *, her agriculture was as flourishing, her manufacturers as numerous and as fully employed, and her commerce as extensive, as they had ever been before.—The capital, therefore, which supported all those different branches of industry, must have been equal to what it had ever been before. — Since the peace, agriculture has been still further improved, the rents of houses have risen in every town and village of the country, a proof of the increasing wealth

* It has proved more expensive than any of our former wars; and has involved us in an additional debt of more than *one hundred millions!* During a profound peace of eleven years, little more than *ten millions* of debt was paid; during a war of seven years, more than *one hundred millions* was contracted.

and revenue of the people; and the annual amount of the greater part of the old taxes, of the principal branches of the excise and customs in particular, has been continually increasing; an equally clear proof of an increasing consumption, and consequently of an increasing produce, which could alone support that consumption.—GREAT BRITAIN *seems to support with ease, a burden which, half a century ago, nobody believed her capable of supporting.*—LET US NOT, HOWEVER, UPON THIS ACCOUNT RASHLY CONCLUDE THAT SHE IS CAPABLE OF SUPPORTING ANY BURDEN; NOR EVEN BE TOO CONFIDENT THAT SHE COULD SUPPORT, WITHOUT GREAT DISTRESS, A BURDEN A LITTLE GREATER THAN WHAT HAS ALREADY BEEN LAID UPON HER *.

* Adam Smith.

SECT.

SECT. VI.

ON WAR.

In *ancient times*, men went to war without much ceremony or pretence: it was thought reafon good enough to juftify the deed, *if one man liked what another man had*; and *war* and *robbery* were the *honourable* profeffions; nothing was *difhonourable* but the arts of *peace* and *induftry*; this is Herodotus's account of the manner of living of the *barbarians* of *Thrace*: and this, with very fmall alterations, might ferve to characterife *all other barbarians*, either of *ancient* or *modern times*.

But at prefent, *we*, who choofe to call ourfelves *civilized nations*, generally affect a more *ceremonious parade*, and *many pretences*.—Complaints are firft made of fome injury received, fome right violated, fome encroachment, detention, or ufurpation, *and none will acknowledge themfelves the aggreffors*; nay, a folemn appeal is made to

HEAVEN for the *truth* of *each assertion*, and the FINAL AVENGER OF THE OPPRESSED, and SEARCHER OF ALL HEARTS, is called upon *to maintain* the *righteous cause*, and to *punish* the *wrong-doer*.—Thus it is with *both parties*; and while *neither* of them will own the *true motives*, perhaps it is *apparent to all the world*, that, on *one side*, if not on *both*, A THIRST OF GLORY, A LUST OF DOMINION, THE CABALS OF STATESMEN, OR THE RAVENOUS APPETITES OF INDIVIDUALS FOR POWER OR PLUNDER, FOR WEALTH WITHOUT INDUSTRY, AND GREATNESS WITHOUT TRUE MERIT, *were the only real and genuine springs of action.*

Now the aims of *princes* in these wars are partly the *same* with, and partly *different* from, those of their *subjects*; as far as RENOWN is concerned, their views are *alike*, for heroism is the wish and envy of all mankind; and to be a nation of heroes, under the conduct of an heroic leader, is regarded both by prince and people, as the summit of all earthly happiness.

It is really astonishing to think with what applause and eclat the feats of such inhuman monsters are transmitted down, in all the pomp of prose and verse, to distant generations: nay, let a prince but feed his subjects with the empty diet of military fame, it matters not what he does besides, in

regard

regard to themſelves as well as others; for the lives and liberties, and every thing that can render ſociety a bleſſing, are willingly offered up as a ſacrifice to this idol, GLORY.—Were the fact to be examined into, you would find, perhaps without *a ſingle exception*, that the *greateſt conquerors abroad* have proved the *heavieſt tyrants at home.*—However, as *victory*, like charity, covereth a multitude of ſins, thus it comes to paſs that reaſonable beings will be content to be *ſlaves themſelves*, provided they may *enſlave others*; and while the people can look up to the glorious hero on the throne, they will be *dazzled* with the ſplendour that ſurrounds him, and forget the deeds of the oppreſſor.

Now, from this view of things, one would be tempted to imagine, that a practice ſo univerſally prevailing was founded in the courſe and conſtitution of nature.—One would be tempted to ſuppoſe, that mankind were created *on purpoſe* to be engaged in deſtructive wars, and to worry and devour one another.—And yet, when we examine into this affair, neither REASON nor EXPERIENCE will give the leaſt countenance to this ſuppoſition.

The REASON of the thing we will conſider now, and reſerve THE FACT till by and by.—Thus, for example, the inhabitants of one county, or one city, have not ſo much as an idea, that A BEING OVERFLOWING WITH BENEVOLENCE has made them the conſtitutional foes of another county or city under the *ſame* government: nor do we at all conceive, that this or that particular town, or diſtrict, can grow rich, or proſper, only by the diſtricts or towns around it being reduced to poverty, or made a dreary waſte.—*On the contrary*, we naturally conclude, and juſtly too, that their intereſts are inſeparable from our own: and were their numbers to be diminiſhed, or their circumſtances altered from affluence to want, we ourſelves, in the rotation of things, ſhould ſoon feel the bad effects of ſuch a change.

If, therefore, this is the caſe with reſpect to *human governments*; and if *they*, notwithſtanding all their faults and failings, can regulate matters ſo much for the better; how then comes it to paſs, that we ſhould aſcribe ſo much imperfection, ſuch want of benevolence, ſuch partiality, nay, ſuch premeditated miſchief, to that great and equal government which preſideth *over all?*—Is it, do you think, that ALMIGHTY GOD cannot make two large diſtricts, *France* and *England* for example, happy but by the miſery of the other?—Or is it, that he has ſo egregiouſly blundered in the firſt framing the conſtitution of things as to render thoſe exploits, called *Wars*, neceſſary

neceſſary for the good of the whole under *his* adminiſtration, which you would juſtly conſider to be a diſgrace to *yours*, and ſeverely puniſh as an outrage?—Surely no; and we cannot, without blaſphemy, aſcribe that conduct to THE BEST OF BEINGS, which is almoſt *too bad* to be ſuppoſed of the *worſt*: ſurely it is much more conſonant to the dictates of unbiaſſed reaſon to believe, *that* OUR COMMON PARENT, *and* UNIVERSAL LORD, *regards all his children and ſubjects with an eye of equal tenderneſs and good-will; and to be firmly perſuaded, that in his plan of government the political intereſt of nations cannot be repugnant to thoſe moral duties of humanity and love, which he has ſo univerſally preſcribed.*—So much as to THE REASON of the thing: let us now conſider the FACT, and be determined by experience.

Princes expect to get by ſucceſsful wars, and a ſeries of conqueſts, either *more territory*, or *more ſubjects*, or a *more ample revenue*; or perhaps, which is generally the caſe, they expect to obtain all three.

1. Now, in regard to TERRITORY, if mere ſuperficies were the thing to be aimed at, it muſt be allowed, that a country of a million of ſquare miles is more in *quantity* than one of half that extent.—But if countries are not to be valued by acres, but by the *cultivation* and the *pro-*

duce

duce of those acres, then it follows, that *ten acres* may be better than a *thousand*, or perhaps *ten thousand* *.

2. As to NUMBERS OF SUBJECTS, surely war and conquest are not the most likely means of attaining this end; and a scheme, which consists in the destruction of the human species, is a very strange one indeed to be proposed for their increase and multiplication; nay, granting that numbers of subjects might be acquired, together with the accession of territory, still these new subjects would add no real strength to the state; because new acquisitions would require more numerous defences, and because a people scattered over an immense tract of country are, in fact, much weaker than half their num-

* My notion of national improvement, security, and happiness, tends not so much to the extending of our commerce, or increasing the number of our manufactures, as to the encouragement of an hardy and, comparatively speaking, innocent race of peasants, *by making corn to grow on millions of acres of land, where none has ever grown before.* From a late computation of Sir JOHN SINCLAIR, it appears that in Great Britain there are 22,351,000 acres of waste land. Let us but once have as many Britons in the kingdom, as the lands of Great Britain are able to sustain, and we shall have little to regret in the loss of *America*; nothing to apprehend from the *partitioning* policy of all the continental despots in Europe. I enter not into the question concerning the population of the country: for whatever may be the present number of the inhabitants of Great Britain, there is no one who has thought upon the subject, but must admit, THAT WERE OUR LANDS BROUGHT TO THEIR PROPER STATE OF CULTIVATION, THEY WOULD AFFORD MAINTENANCE TO TWICE AS MANY AS AT PRESENT EXIST IN THIS COUNTRY. *The Bishop of Landaff.*

bers

bers acting in concert together, and able by their vicinity to ſuccour one another.

Moreover, as to the affair of THE REVENUE, and the produce of taxes, the ſame arguments conclude equally ſtrong in this caſe as in the former: and the indiſputable fact is, that an ill-peopled country, though large and extenſive, neither produces ſo great a revenue as a ſmall one well cultivated and populous: nor if it did, would the neat produce of ſuch a revenue be equal to that of the other, becauſe it is, in a manner, ſwallowed up in *governments*, *guards*, and *garriſons*, in *ſalaries* and *penſions*, and all the concurring *perquiſites* and *expences* attendant on *diſtant provinces*.

In reference to the views of the people; as far as ſuch views coincide with thoſe of the prince, ſo they have been conſidered already: but ſeeing that the thirſt of inordinate riches in private ſubjects, which puſhes them on to wiſh ſo vehemently for war, has ſomething in it diſtinct from *the avarice of princes*; let us now examine, whether this trade of war is a likely method to make a people *rich*, and let us conſider every plea that can be offered.—" Surely, ſay theſe men, to return home laden " with the ſpoils of wealthy nations is a compendious " way of getting wealth; ſurely we cannot be deceived "in ſo plain a caſe: for we ſee that what has been ga-"thering together and accumulating for years, and per-"haps for ages, thus becomes our own at once; and "more might be acquired by a happy victory within the "compaſs of a day, perhaps of an hour, than we could "otherwiſe promiſe to ourſelves by the tedious purſuits "of induſtry through the whole courſe of a long labo-"rious life."

Now, in order to treat with this people in their own way, I would not awake them out of their preſent golden dream; I would therefore ſuppoſe, that they might ſucceed to their hearts deſire, though there is a chance at leaſt of being diſappointed, and of meeting with captivity inſtead of conqueſt: I will wave likewiſe all conſiderations drawn from the intoxicating nature of riches, when ſo rapidly got, and improperly acquired: I will alſo grant, that great ſtores of gold and ſilver, of jewels, diamonds, and precious ſtones, may be brought home; and yet the treaſures of the univerſe may, if you pleaſe, be made to circulate within the limits of our own little country: and if this were not enough, I would ſtill grant more, did I really know what could be wiſhed for or expected more.

The *ſoldier of fortune*, being made thus *rich*, ſits down

to

to enjoy the fruits of his conqueſt, and to gratify his wiſhes after ſo much fatigue and toil: but, alas! he preſently finds, that *in proportion* as this heroical ſpirit and thirſt for glory have diffuſed themſelves among his countrymen, in *the ſame proportion* as *the ſpirit of induſtry hath ſunk and died away*; *every neceſſary and every comfort and elegance of life are grown dearer than before, becauſe there are fewer hands and leſs inclination to produce them*; *at the ſame time his own deſires, and artificial wants, inſtead of being leſſened, are greatly multiplied*; *for of what uſe are riches to him, unleſs enjoyed?*—Thus, therefore, it comes to paſs, that his heaps of treaſure are like the ſnow in ſummer, continually melting away; ſo that *the land of heroes* ſoon becomes *the country of beggars.*—His riches, it is true, ruſhed in upon him like a flood: but, as he had no means of retaining them, every article he wanted or wiſhed for, drained away his ſtores like the holes in a ſieve, till the bottom became quite dry: in ſhort, in this ſituation the ſums, which are daily and hourly iſſuing out, are not to be replaced but by *a new war*, and *a new ſeries* of *victories*; and *theſe new wars* and *new victories* do all enhance the *former evils*; ſo that the relative poverty of the inhabitants of this warlike country becomes ſo much the greater, in proportion to

 their

their ſucceſs, in the very means miſtakenly propoſed for enriching them.

A few, indeed, incited by the ſtrong inſtinct of an avaricious temper, may gather and ſcrape up what the many are ſquandering away; and ſo the impoveriſhment of the community may become the enrichment of the individual.—But it is utterly impoſſible, that the great majority of any country can grow wealthy by that courſe of life, which renders them both very extravagant, and very idle.

To illuſtrate this train of reaſoning, let us have recourſe to FACTS: but let the facts be ſuch as my opponents in this argument would wiſh, of all others, to have produced on this occaſion: and as the example of the ROMANS is eternally quoted, from the pamphleteer in the garret, to the patriot in the ſenate, as extremely worthy of the imitation of BRITONS; let their example decide the diſpute.—" The brave Romans! That glo-" rious! that god-like people! The conquerors of the " world! who made the moſt haughty nations to ſub-" mit! who put the wealthieſt under tribute, and " brought all the riches of the univerſe to center in the " imperial city of Rome!"

Now *this people*, at the beginning of their ſtate, had a territory not ſo large as one of our middling counties,

and

and neither healthy nor fertile in its nature; yet, by means of frugality and induſtry, they not only procured a comfortable ſubſiſtence, but alſo were enabled to carry on their petty wars without burden to the ſtate, or pay to the troops; each huſbandman or little freeholder ſerving *gratis*, and providing his own clothes and arms during the ſhort time that was neceſſary for him to be abſent from his cottage and family on ſuch expeditions.

But when their neighbours were all ſubdued, and *the ſeat of war* removed to more *diſtant countries*, it became impoſſible for them to draw their ſubſiſtence from their own farms; or, in other words, to ſerve *gratis any longer*; and therefore they were under a neceſſity to accept of *pay*. —Moreover, as they could ſeldom viſit their little eſtates, theſe farms were unavoidably neglected, and conſequently were ſoon diſpoſed of to engroſſing purchaſers: and *thus it came to paſs that the lands about Rome were monopolized into a few hands by dint of their very conqueſts and ſucceſſes*: and thus alſo *the ſpirit of induſtry* began to decline, in proportion as *the military genius* gained the aſcendant.—A proof of this we have in LIVY, even ſo far back as the time of their laſt king *Tarquinius Superbus*: for one of the complaints brought againſt that prince

prince was couched in the following terms, that having employed his ſoldiers in making drains and common ſewers, "*they thought it an high diſgrace to warriors to be* "*treated as mechanics, and that the conquerors of the neigh-* "*bouring nations ſhould be degraded into ſtone-cutters and* "*maſons*," though theſe works are not *the monuments of unmeaning folly*, or the works of *oſtentation*, but evidently calculated for *the health* of the citizens, and *the convenience* of the public.—*Had he led forth theſe indignant heroes to the extirpation of ſome neighbouring ſtate, they would not have conſidered that as a diſhonour to their character.*

But to proceed: the genius of ROME being formed for war, the Romans puſhed their conqueſts over nations ſtill more remote: but alas! the *Quirites*, the body of the people, were ſo far from reaping any advantage from theſe new triumphs, that they generally found themſelves to be poorer at the end of their moſt glorious wars than before they began them.—At the cloſe of each ſucceſsful war it was cuſtomary to divide a part of the lands of the vanquiſhed among the veteran ſoldiers, and to grant them a diſmiſſion in order to cultivate their new acquiſitions.—But ſuch eſtates being *far diſtant from the city*, became in fact ſo much the leſs valuable; and the

new

new proprietor had lefs inclination than ever to forfake the capital, and to banifh himfelf to thefe diftant provinces.—(For here let it be noted, that Rome was become, by this time, the theatre of pleafure, as well as the feat of empire, where all who wifhed to act a part on the ftage of ambition, popularity, or politics; all who wanted to be engaged in fcenes of debauchery, or intrigues of ftate; all, in fhort, who had any thing to fpend, or any thing to expect, made Rome their rendezvous, and reforted thither as to a common mart).—This being the cafe, it is not at all furprifing, that thefe late acquifitions were deferted and fold for a very trifle; nor is it any wonder, that the mafs of the Roman people fhould be fo immerfed in debt, as we find by their own hiftorians they continually were, when we reflect, that their military life indifpofed them for agriculture or manufactures, and that their notions of conqueft and of glory rendered them extravagant, prodigal, and vain.

However, in this manner they went on, continuing to extend their victories and their triumphs; and after the triumph, fubfifting for a while by the fale of the lands above mentioned, or by their fhares in the divifion of the booty: but when thefe were fpent, as they quickly were, then they fush ſunk into a more wretched ſtate of poverty than before, eagerly wiſhing for a new war as the only means of repairing their deſperate fortunes, and clamouring againſt every perſon that would dare to appear as an advocate for peace: and thus they increaſed their ſufferings inſtead of removing them.

At laſt they ſubdued the world, as far as it was known at that time, or thought worth ſubduing, and then both the tribute and the plunder of the univerſe were imported into *Rome*; then, therefore, the bulk of the inhabitants of that city muſt have been exceedingly wealthy, had wealth conſiſted in heaps of gold and ſilver; and then likewiſe, if ever, the bleſſings of victory muſt have been felt, had it been capable of producing any.— *But alas! whatever riches a few grandees, the leaders of armies, the governors of provinces, the minions of the populace, or the harpies of oppreſſion, might have amaſſed together, the great majority of the people were poor and miſerable beyond expreſſion: and while the vain wretches were ſtrutting with pride, and elated with inſolence, as the maſters of the world, they had no other means of ſubſiſting, when peace was made and their prize-money ſpent, than to receive a kind of alms in corn from the public granaries, or to carry about their bread-baſkets, and beg from door to*

 door.

door.—Moreover, ſuch among them as had chanced to have a piece of land left unmortgaged, or ſomething valuable to pledge, found, to their ſorrow, that the intereſt of money (being hardly ever leſs than twelve *per cent.* and frequently more) would ſoon eat up their little ſubſtance, and reduce them to an equality with the reſt of their illuſtrious brother beggars.—*Nay, ſo extremely low was the credit of theſe maſters of the world, that they were truſted with the payment of their intereſt no longer than from month to month;—than which there cannot be a more glaring proof, both of the abject poverty, and of the cheating diſpoſitions of theſe heroic citizens of imperial Rome.*—Now this being the UNDOUBTED FACT, every humane and benevolent man, far from conſidering theſe people as objects worthy of imitation, will look upon them with a juſt abhorrence and indignation; and every wiſe ſtate, conſulting the good of the whole, will take warning by their fatal example, and ſtifle, as much as poſſible, the very beginning of ſuch a *Roman ſpirit* in its ſubjects.

The caſe of the *ancient Romans* having thus been conſidered at large, leſs may be requiſite as to what is to follow.—AND THEREFORE SUFFICE IT TO OBSERVE, THAT THE WARS OF EUROPE FOR THESE TWO HUNDRED YEARS LAST PAST, BY THE CONFESSION

OF ALL PARTIES, HAVE REALLY ENDED IN THE ADVANTAGE OF NONE, BUT TO THE MANIFEST DETRIMENT OF ALL.—SUFFICE IT FARTHER TO REMARK, THAT HAD EACH OF THE CONTENDING POWERS EMPLOYED THEIR SUBJECTS IN CULTIVATING AND IMPROVING SUCH LANDS AS WERE CLEAR OF ALL DISPUTED TITLES, INSTEAD OF AIMING AT MORE EXTENDED POSSESSIONS, THEY HAD CONSULTED BOTH THEIR OWN AND THEIR PEOPLE'S GREATNESS MUCH MORE EFFICACIOUSLY, THAN BY ALL THE VICTORIES OF A CÆSAR OR AN ALEXANDER.

Upon the whole, therefore, it is evident to a demonſtration, that nothing can reſult from ſuch ſyſtems as theſe, however ſpecious and plauſible in appearance, but *diſappointment*, *want*, and *beggary.—For the great laws of* PROVIDENCE, *and the courſe of nature, are not to be reverſed or counteracted by the feeble efforts of wayward man, nor will the rules of ſound politics ever bear a ſeparation from thoſe of true and genuine morality.*—Not to mention, that the *victors themſelves* will experience it to their coſts, ſooner or later, that in *vanquiſhing others* they are only *preparing a more magnificent tomb* for the interment of their *liberty*.

In very deed the *good providence* of GOD hath, as it were,

were, taken *peculiar pains* to preclude mankind from having *any plausible pretence* for pursuing either *this* or *any other scheme of depopulation.*—And the traces of such *preventing endeavours*, if I may so speak, are perfectly legible both in the natural, and in the moral worlds.

In the natural world, our bountiful CREATOR *hath formed different* SOILS, *and appointed different* CLIMATES, *whereby the inhabitants of different countries may supply each other with their respective fruits and products, so that by exciting a reciprocal industry, they may carry on an intercourse mutually beneficial, and universally benevolent.*

Nay more, even where there is no remarkable difference of soil or of climates, we find a great difference of TALENTS; and, if I may be allowed the expression, a wonderful variety of strata in the human mind.—Thus, for example, the alteration of latitude between *Norwich* and *Manchester*, and the variation of soil, are not worth naming; moreover, the materials made use of in both places, wool, flax, and silk, are just the same; yet *so different* are the productions of their respective looms, that countries which are thousands of miles apart could hardly exhibit a greater contrast.—Now had *Norwich* and *Manchester* been the capitals of two neighbouring kingdoms, instead of *love* and *union*, we should have heard of nothing but *jealousies* and *wars*; each would have prognosticated, that the flourishing state of the one portended the downfal of the other; each would have had their respective complaints, uttered in the most doleful accents, concerning their own loss of trade, and of the formidable progress of their rivals; and, if the respective governments were in any degree popular, *each* would have had a set of *patriots* and *orators* closing their inflammatory harangues with a DELENDA EST CARTHAGO.—" We must destroy our rivals, our competi-" tors and commercial enemies, or be destroyed by " them; for our interests are opposite, and can never " coincide."—And yet, notwithstanding all these *canting phrases*, it is as clear as the meridian sun, that in case these cities had belonged to different kingdoms *(France* and *England* for example) there would then have been no more need for either of them to have gone to war than there is at present.

In short, if mankind would but open their eyes, they might plainly see, that there is no one argument for inducing different nations to fight for the sake of trade, but which would equally oblige every country, town, village, nay, and every shop among ourselves, to be engaged in civil and intestine wars for the same end: nor, on the contrary, is there any motive

motive of interest or advantage that can be urged for restraining the parts of the same government from these unnatural and foolish contests, but which would conclude equally strong against separate and independent nations making war with each other on the like pretext.

Moreover, the instinct of curiosity, and the thirst of novelty, which are so universally implanted in human nature, whereby various nations and different people so ardently wish to be customers to each other, is another proof that the curious manufactures of one nation will never want a vent among the richer inhabitants of another, provided they are reasonably *cheap* and *good*; so that the richer one nation is, the more it has to spare, and the more it will certainly lay out on the produce and manufactures of its ingenious neighbour.—Do you object to this? *Do you envy the wealth, or repine at the prosperity, of the nations around you?*—If *you do*, consider what is *the consequence*, viz. that you *wish to keep a shop*, but *hope to have only* BEGGARS *for your customers.*

As to the moral and political world, PROVIDENCE has so ordained, that every nation may increase in *frugality* and *industry*, and consequently in *riches*, if they please; because it has given a power to every nation to make good laws, and wise regulations, for their internal

government:

government: and none can juſtly blame them on this account.—Should, for example, the POLES, or the TARTARS, grow weary of their preſent wretched ſyſtems, and reſolve upon a better conſtitution; ſhould they prefer employment to ſloth, liberty to ſlavery, and trade and manufactures to theft and robbery; ſhould they give all poſſible freedom and encouragement to induſtrious artificers, and lay heavy diſcouragements on idleneſs and vice, by means of judicious taxes; and laſtly, ſhould they root out all notions of beggarly pride, and of the glory of making marauding incurſions;—what a mighty, what a happy change would ſoon appear in the face of thoſe countries!—And what could then be ſaid to be wanting in order to render ſuch nations truly *rich* and *great*?

Perhaps ſome neighbouring ſtate (entertaining a fooliſh jealouſy) would take the alarm, that their trade was in danger.—But if they attempted to invade ſuch a kingdom, they would find, to their coſt, that an induſtrious ſtate, abounding with people and with riches, having its magazines well ſtored, its frontier towns well fortified, the garriſons duly paid, and the whole country full of villages and encloſures; I ſay, they would feel to their coſt, that ſuch a ſtate is the ſtrongeſt of all others, and the moſt difficult to be ſubdued: not to mention that other potentates would naturally riſe up for its defence and preſervation; becauſe, indeed, it would be for their intereſt that ſuch a ſtate as this ſhould not be ſwallowed up by another, and becauſe they themſelves might have *many things* to *hope* from it, and *nothing* to *fear*.

But is this ſpell, this witchcraft of the jealouſy of trade never to be diſſolved? And are there no hopes that mankind will recover their ſenſes as to theſe things?—For of all abſurdities, that of going to war for the ſake of getting trade is the moſt abſurd; and nothing in nature can be ſo extravagantly fooliſh.

Perhaps you cannot digeſt this; you do not believe it.—Be it ſo.—Grant, therefore, that you ſubdue your rival by force of arms: will that circumſtance render your goods *cheaper* at market than they were before?—And if it will not, nay if it tends to render them much dearer, what have you got by ſuch a victory?—I aſk further, what will be the conduct of foreign nations, when your goods are brought to their markets?—They will not inquire, whether you were victorious or not; but only, whether you will ſell *cheaper*, or at leaſt as *cheap* as others?—Try and ſee, whether any perſons, or any nations, ever yet proceeded upon any other plan; and

and if they never did, and never can be ſuppoſed to do ſo, then it is evident to a demonſtration, that trade will always follow *cheapneſs*, and not *conqueſt*.—Nay, conſider how it is with yourſelves at home: do *heroes* and *bruiſers* get *more cuſtomers* to their ſhops, *becauſe* they are *heroes* and *bruiſers*; or would not you yourſelf rather deal with a *feeble perſon*, who will *uſe you well*, than with a *brother hero*, ſhould *he demand a higher price*?

Now *all theſe facts* are ſo very *notorious*, that none can diſpute the truth of them.—And throughout the hiſtories of all countries, and of all ages, there is not a ſingle example to the contrary.

JUDGE, THEREFORE, FROM WHAT HAS BEEN SAID, WHETHER ANY ONE ADVANTAGE CAN BE OBTAINED TO SOCIETY, EVEN BY THE MOST SUCCESSFUL WARS, THAT MAY NOT BE INCOMPARABLY GREATER, AND MORE EASILY PROCURED, BY THE ARTS OF PEACE.

As to thoſe who are always clamouring for war, and ſounding the alarm to battle, let us conſider who they are, and what are their motives; and then it will be no difficult matter to determine concerning the deference that

ought

ought to be paid to their *opinions*, and the merit of their *patriotic zeal*.

1. The firſt on the liſt here in *Britain* (for different countries have different ſorts of firebrands), I ſay the firſt here in Britain is the *mock patriot* and *furious anti-courtier* —He always begins with ſchemes of œconomy, and a zealous promoter of national frugality.—He loudly declaims againſt even a ſmall, annual, parliamentary army, both on account of its expence, and its danger; and pretends to be ſtruck with a panic at every red coat that he ſees.—By perſevering in theſe laudable endeavours, and by ſowing the ſeeds of jealouſy and diſtruſt among the ignorant and unwary, he prevents ſuch a number of forces, by ſea and land, from being kept up, as are prudently neceſſary for the common ſafety of the kingdom: this is one ſtep gained.—In the next place, after having thrown out ſuch a tempting bait for foreigners to catch at, on any trifling account he is all on fire; his breaſt beats high with the love of his country, and his ſoul breathes vengeance againſt the foes of Britain: every popular topic, and every inflammatory harangue is immediately put into rehearſal; and, O liberty! O my country! is the continual theme.—The fire then ſpreads; the ſouls of the noble Britons are enkindled at

it, and *vengeance* and *war* are immediately resolved upon. —Then the ministry are all in a hurry and a flutter; new levies are half formed and half disciplined; squadrons at sea half manned, and the officers mere novices in their business.—In short, ignorance, unskilfulness, and confusion, are unavoidable for a time; the necessary consequence of which is some defeat received, some stain or dishonour cast upon the arms of Britain.—*Then the long wished for opportunity comes at last; the patriot roars, the populace clamour and address, the ministry tremble, and the administration sinks.*—The ministerial throne now being vacant, he triumphantly ascends it, *adopts* those measures he had formerly *condemned*, reaps the benefit of the preparations and plans of his predecessor, and, in the natural course of things, very probably gains some advantages.—This restores the credit of the arms of Britain. —"Now the lion is roused, and now is the time for "crushing our enemies, that they may never be able to "rise again."—This is pretext enough; and thus the nation is plunged into an expence ten times as great, and made to raise forces twenty times as numerous, as were complained of before. "However, being now victorious, "let us follow the blow, and manfully go on, and let "neither expence of blood nor of treasure be at all re-

 "garded;

" garded; for another campaign will undoubtedly bring " the enemy to ſubmit to our own terms, and it is im- " poſſible that they ſhould ſtand out any longer."— Well, another campaign is fought...... and another...... and another...... and another, and yet the enemy holds out; nor is the cart blanche making any progreſs in its journey into Britain.—A peace at laſt is made; the terms of it are unpopular.—Schemes of *exceſſive œconomy* are called for by a new ſet of patriots; and the ſame arts are played off to dethrone the reigning miniſter, which he had practiſed to dethrone his predeceſſor.—And thus the *patriotic farce* goes round and round; and it were well did not eloquence too often gull the *independent* or *ruling members* of our ſenate, and thus produce a real and bloody tragedy to our country and mankind.

2. The next in this liſt is the *hungry pamphleteer*, who writes for bread.—The miniſtry will not retain him on their ſide, *therefore* he muſt write againſt them, and do as much miſchief as he can in order to be bought off.— At the worſt, a pillory or a proſecution is a never-failing remedy againſt a political author's ſtarving; nay, perhaps it may get him a penſion or a place at laſt: in the interim, the province of this creature is to be a kind of *jackall* to the *patriot lion*; for he beats the foreſt, and

 firſt

first ſtarts the game; he explores the reigning humour and whim of *the populace*, and by frequent trials diſcovers the part where the miniſtry are moſt vulnerable.—But, above all, he never fails to put the mob in the mind, of what indeed they believed before, *that politics is a ſubject which every one underſtands*....EXCEPT—*the miniſtry*, and that nothing is ſo eaſy as to bring the king of France to ſue for peace on his knees at the bar of a Britiſh houſe of commons, were—ſuch——and ſuch——at the helm, as honeſt and uncorrupt as they ought to be. This is delightful; and this, with the old ſtories of Agincourt and Creſſy, regales, nay intoxicates the mob, and inſpires them with an enthuſiaſm bordering upon madneſs.—The ſame ideas return; the former battles are fought over again; and we have already taken poſſeſſion of the gates of Paris in the warmth of a frantic imagination; though it is certain that even were this circumſtance ever to happen, we ourſelves ſhould be the greateſt loſers; for the conqueſt of France by England, in the event of things, would come to the ſame point as the conqueſt of England by France; becauſe the ſeat of empire would be transferred to the greater kingdom, and the leſſer would be made a province to it.

3. Near akin to this man, is that other monſter of modern times, who is perpetually declaiming againſt a peace,

peace, viz. *the broker*, and *the gambler of Change-alley.* Letters from the Hague, wrote in a garret at home for half a guinea;... the first news of a battle fought (it matters not how improbable) with a list of the slain and prisoners, their cannon, colours, &c...... great firings heard at sea between squadrons not yet out of port;.... a town taken before the enemy was near it;.... an intercepted letter that never was wrote;.... a forged gazette;.... or, in short, any thing else that will elate or depress the minds of the undiscerning multitude, serves the purpose of the bear or the bull, to sink or raise the price of stocks, according as he wishes either to buy or sell, and by these vile means the wretch, who perhaps the other day came up to London in the waggon to be an under clerk or message boy in a warehouse, acquires such a fortune as sets him on a par with the greatest nobles of the land.

4. The *news writers* are a fourth species of political firebrand: a species which abound in this country more than in any other; for as men are in this kingdom allowed greater liberty to say, or write, what they please; so likewise is *the abuse* of that blessing carried to a higher pitch.—In fact these people may be truly said to *trade in blood:* for a war is their harvest; and a bloody battle

produces

produces a crop of an hundred fold: how then can it be ſuppoſed that they can ever become the friends of peace?—And how can you expect that any miniſters can be their favourites, but the miniſters of death?—Yet theſe are the men who may be truly ſaid to govern the minds of the good people of England, and to turn their affections whitherſoever they pleaſe; who can render any ſcheme unpopular which they diſlike, and whoſe approbation or frown are regarded by thouſands, and almoſt by millions, as the ſtandard of right and wrong, of truth or falſehood; for it is a fact, an indiſputable fact, that this country is as much news-mad and news-ridden now, as ever it was popery-mad or prieſt-ridden in the days of our forefathers.

5. The *jobbers* and *contractors of all kinds* and *of all degrees* for our *fleets* and *armies*:—the clerks and pay-maſters in the ſeveral departments belonging to war:.... and every other agent, who has the fingering of the *public money*, may be ſaid to conſtitute a diſtinct brood of *vultures*, who prey upon their *own ſpecies*, and fatten upon *human gore*.—It would be endleſs to recount the various arts and ſtratagems by which this tribe of devourers have amaſſed to themſelves aſtoniſhing riches from very ſlender beginnings, through the continuance and extent of the

war;

war; confequently, as long as any profpect could remain of fqueezing fomewhat more out of the pockets of an *exhaufted*, but *infatuated people*; fo long the *war-hoop* would be the cry of thefe inhuman favages; and fo long would they ftart and invent objections to every propofition that could be made for the reftoring peace.....because government bills would yet bear fome price in the alley, and omnium and fcrip would ftill fell at market.

6. *Many* of *the dealers* in *exports* and *imports*, and *feveral* of *the traders in the colonies*, are too often found to be affiftants in promoting the cry for every new war: and when war is undertaken, in preventing any overtures towards a peace.—You do not fathom the depth of this policy; you are not capable to comprehend it.—Alas! it is but too eafily explained; and, when explained, but too well proved from experience.—*The general intereft of trade*, and *the intereft of particular traders*, are *very diftinct things*; nay, are very often *quite oppofite* to each other.—The intereft of general trade arifes from *general induftry*; and therefore can only be promoted by the arts of peace: but the misfortune is, that during a peace the prices of goods feldom fluctuate, and there are few or no opportunities of getting fuddenly rich.—A

war,

war, on the contrary, unſettles all things, and opens a wide field for *ſpeculations*; therefore a lucky hit, or the engroſſing a commodity, when there is but little at market.....A rich capture.....or a ſmuggling, I ſhould rather ſay, a traiterous, intercourſe with the enemy, ſometimes by bribes to governors and officers, and ſometimes through other channels:—or, perhaps, the hopes of coming in for *a ſhare* in *a lucrative job*, or a *public contract*; theſe, and many ſuch like notable expedients, are cheriſhed by the warmth of war, like plants in a hot-bed; but they are chilled by the cold languid circulation of peaceful induſtry.

This being the caſe, the warlike zeal of theſe men, and their declamations againſt all reconciliatory meaſures, are but too eaſily accounted for; and while the dulcis amor lucri is the governing principle of trade, what other conduct are you to expect?

But what if the men of *landed property*, and the numerous band of *Engliſh artificers* and *manufacturers*, who conſtitute, beyond all doubt, the great body of the kingdom, and whoſe real intereſt muſt be on the ſide of peace; what if *they* ſhould not be as military in their diſpoſition as theſe gentlemen would wiſh they were?—Why then all arts muſt be uſed, and indefatigable pains

be

be taken to perſuade them, that *this particular war* is calculated for their benefit; and that the conqueſt of ſuch or ſuch a place would infallibly redound both to the advantage of the landed intereſts, and the improvement and extenſion of manufactures.—" Should (for ex-" ample) the Engliſh once become maſters of CANADA, " the importation of ſkins and beavers, and the manu-" facture of fine hats, would extend prodigiouſly; every " man might afford to wear a beaver hat if he pleaſed, " and every woman be decorated in the richeſt furs; in " return for which our coarſe woollens would find ſuch " a vent throughout our immenſe northern regions, as " would make ample ſatisfaction for all our expences." Well, *Canada* is taken, and is now all our own; but what is the conſequence, after a trial of ſome years poſſeſſion, let thoſe declare who can, and as they were before ſo laviſh in their promiſes, let them at laſt prove their aſſertions, by appealing to fact and experience.— Alas! they cannot do it: nay, ſo far from it, that beaver, and furs, and hats, are *dearer than ever*: and all the woollens, which have been conſumed in thoſe countries by the *native inhabitants*, do hardly amount to a greater quantity than thoſe very ſoldiers and ſailors would have worn and consumed, who were lost in the taking, defending, and garrisoning of those countries.

" However, if Canada did not answer our sanguine
" expectations, sure we were, that the sugar countries
" would make amends for all: and, therefore, if the im-
" portant islands of GAUDALOUPE and MARTINICO
" were to be subdued, then sugars, and coffee, and cho-
" colate, and indigo, and cotton, &c. &c. would become
" as cheap as we could wish; and both the country gen-
" tleman and the manufacturer would find their account
" in such conquests as these." Well, *Gaudaloupe* and *Martinico* are both taken, and many other islands besides are added to our empire, whose produce is the very same with theirs.—*Yet, what elegance of life, or what ingredient for manufacture, is thereby become the cheaper? and which of all these things can be purchased at a lower rate at present than before the war?*—Not one can be named.—On the contrary, the man of landed property can tell but too circumstantially, that *taxes* are risen higher than ever—that the interest of money is greater—that every additional load of national debt is a new mortgage on his exhausted and impoverished estate—and that, if he happens to be a member of parliament, he runs the risk of

being

being bought out of his family borough, by ſome upſtart gambler, jobber, or contractor.

The *Engliſh manufacturer* likewiſe both ſees and feels, that *every foreign material*, of uſe in his trade, is grown *much dearer*,——that all hands are become extremely *ſcarce*, their *wages* prodigiouſly raiſed,—the goods, of courſe, badly and ſcandalouſly manufactured,———and yet *cannot* be afforded at the *ſame price as heretofore*—— that, therefore, the ſale of Engliſh manufactures has greatly decreaſed in foreign countries ſince the commencement of war;——and, what is worſe than all, that induſtry at home is diminiſhed.—All theſe things, I ſay, the *Engliſh manufacturer* both *ſees* and *feels*: and IS NOT THIS ENOUGH?

7. The *land* and *ſea officers* are, of courſe, the invariable advocates for war.—Indeed it is their trade, their bread, and the ſure way to get promotion; therefore no other language can be expected from them: and yet, to do them juſtice, of all the adverſaries of peace, they are the faireſt and moſt open in their proceedings; they uſe no art of colouring, and you know their motive, you muſt allow for it accordingly.

But after all, what have I been doing? and how can

I hope for profelytes by this kind of writing——It is true, in regard to the points attempted to be proved, I have certainly proved them.—" NEITHER PRINCES " NOR PEOPLE CAN BE GAINERS BY THE MOST SUC- " CESSFUL WARS:——TRADE, IN PARTICULAR, WILL " MAKE ITS WAY TO THE COUNTRY WHERE GOODS " ARE MANUFACTURED THE BEST AND CHEAPEST: " —BUT CONQUERING NATIONS NEITHER MANU- " FACTURE WELL NOR CHEAP:—AND CONSEQUENT- " LY MUST SINK IN TRADE IN PROPORTION AS THEY " EXTEND IN CONQUEST."—Thefe things are now inconteftibly clear, if any thing ever was fo.—But, alas! who will thank me for fuch leffons as thefe? The *feven claffes* of men juft enumerated certainly will not; and as to *the mob*, the blood-thirfty mob, no arguments, and no demonftrations whatever, can perfuade them to withdraw their veneration from their grim idol, the god of flaughter.—On the contrary, to knock a man on the head, is to take from him his all at once.—This is a compendious way, and this they underftand.—*But to excite that man* (whom perhaps they have long called their enemy) *to greater induftry and fobriety, to confider him as a cuftomer to them, and themfelves as*

cuftomers

customers to him, so that the richer both are, the better it may be for each other; and, in short, to promote a mutual trade to mutual benefit: this is a kind of reasoning, as unintelligible to their comprehensions as the antipodes themselves *.

SOME FEW, PERHAPS A VERY FEW INDEED, MAY BE STRUCK WITH THE FORCE OF THESE TRUTHS, AND YIELD THEIR MINDS TO CONVICTION.——POSSIBLY IN A LONG COURSE OF TIME THEIR NUMBERS MAY INCREASE—AND POSSIBLY, AT LAST, THE TIDE MAY TURN; SO THAT OUR POSTERITY MAY REGARD THE PRESENT MADNESS OF GOING TO WAR FOR THE SAKE OF TRADE, RICHES, OR DOMINION, WITH THE SAME EYE OF ASTONISHMENT AND PITY, THAT WE DO THE MADNESS OF OUR FOREFATHERS IN FIGHTING UNDER THE BANNER OF THE PEACEFUL CROSS.

* Dean TUCKER.

SECT.

SECT. VII.

ON TAXES.

Before I enter upon the examination of the effects of ſome particular taxes, it may be neceſſary to premiſe the four following maxims with regard to taxes in general.

1. *The ſubjects of every ſtate ought to contribute towards the ſupport of the government, as nearly as poſſible, in proportion to their reſpective abilities*; that is, in proportion to the revenue which they reſpectively enjoy under the protection of the ſtate.—The expence of government to the individuals of a great nation, is like the expence of management to the joint tenants of a great eſtate, who are all obliged to contribute in proportion to their reſpective intereſts in the eſtate.—In the obſervation or neglect of this maxim conſiſts, what is called the EQUALITY OF INEQUALITY of taxation.

2. *The tax which each individual is bound to pay ought*

 to

to be certain.—The *time* of payment, the *manner* of payment, the *quantity* to be paid, ought all to be clear and plain to the contributor, and to every other perſon.—Where it is otherwiſe, every perſon ſubject to the tax is put more or leſs in the power of the tax-gatherer, who can either aggravate the tax upon any obnoxious contributor, or extort, by the terror of ſuch aggravation, ſome preſent or perquiſite to himſelf.—The uncertainty of taxation encourages the inſolence and favours the corruption of an order of men who are naturally unpopular, even where they are neither inſolent nor corrupt.—The certainty of what each individual ought to pay is, in taxation, a matter of ſo great importance, that a very conſiderable degree of *inequality*, it appears, I believe, from the experience of all nations, is not near ſo great an evil as a very ſmall degree of *uncertainty*.

3. *Every tax ought to be levied at the time, or in the manner, in which it is moſt likely to be convenient for the contributor to pay it.*—A tax upon the rent of land or of houſes, payable at the ſame term at which ſuch rents are uſually paid, is levied at the time when it is moſt likely to have wherewithal to pay.—Taxes upon ſuch conſumable goods as are articles of luxury, are all *finally* paid by the

the consumer *, and generally in a manner that is very convenient for him.—He pays them by little and little, as he has occasion to buy the goods.—As he is at liberty too, either to buy, or not to buy, as he pleases, it must be his own fault if he ever suffers any considerable inconveniency from such taxes.

4. *Every tax ought to be so contrived as both to take out*

* It is an opinion, zealously promoted by some political writers, that since all taxes, as they pretend, fall *ultimately* upon *land*, it were better to lay them originally *there*, and abolish every duty upon consumptions. But we deny, that all taxes fall ultimately upon land. If a duty be laid upon any *commodity* consumed by an artisan, he has two obvious expedients for paying it; he may retrench somewhat of his expence, or he may increase his labour. *Both these resources* are *more easy* and *natural*, than *that* of *heightening his wages*. We see that, in years of *scarcity*, the weaver either *consumes less* or *labours more*, or employs both these expedients of frugality and industry, by which he is enabled to reach the end of the year. *By what contrivance can he raise the price of his labour?* The manufacturer who employs him will not give him more: neither can he, because the merchant, who exports the cloth, cannot raise its price, being limited by the price which it yields in foreign markets. Every man, to be sure, is desirous of pushing off from himself the burden of any tax which is imposed, and of laying it upon others: but as every man has the same inclination, and is upon the *defensive*, no set of men can be supposed to prevail altogether in this contest. And why the landed gentleman should be the victim of the whole, and should not be able to defend himself, as well as others are, I cannot readily imagine. All tradesmen, indeed, would willingly prey upon him, and divide him among them, if they could; but this inclination they always have, though no taxes were levied; and the same methods, by which he guards against the imposition of tradesmen before taxes, will serve him afterwards, and make them share the burden with him.—Hume.

and to keep out of the pockets of the people as little as poſſible, over and above what it brings into the public treaſury of the ſtate.—A tax may either take out or keep out of the pockets of the people a great deal more than it brings into the public treaſury, in the four following ways.—FIRST, the levying of it may require a great number of officers, whoſe ſalaries may eat up the greater part of the produce of the tax, and whoſe perquiſites may impoſe another additional tax upon the people.—SECONDLY, it may obſtruct the induſtry of the people, and diſcourage them from applying to certain branches of buſineſs which might give maintenance and employment to great multitudes.—While it obliges the people to pay, it may thus diminiſh, or perhaps deſtroy, ſome of the funds which might enable them more eaſily to do ſo.—THIRDLY, by the forfeitures and other penalties which thoſe unfortunate individuals incur who attempt unſucceſsfully to evade the tax, it may frequently ruin them, and thereby put an end to the benefit which the community might have received from the employment of their capitals.—An injudicious tax offers a great temptation to ſmuggling.—But the penalties of ſmuggling muſt riſe in proportion to the temptation.—The law, contrary to all the ordinary principles of juſtice, firſt creates the temptation, and then punishes those who yield to it; and it commonly enhances the punishment too in proportion to the very circumstance which ought certainly to alleviate it, the temptation to commit the crime *.—Fourthly, by subjecting the people to the frequent visits and the odious examination of the tax-gatherers, it may expose them to much unnecessary trouble, vexation, and oppression; and though vexation is not, strictly speaking, expence, it is certainly equivalent to the expence at which every man would be willing to redeem himself from it.

It is in some one or other of these four different ways that taxes are frequently so much more burdensome to the people than they are beneficial to the sovereign.

The best taxes are such as are levied upon *consumptions*, especially those of *luxury*; because such taxes are least felt by the people.—They seem, in some measure, voluntary; since a man may choose how far he will use the commodity which is taxed: they are paid gradually and insensibly: they naturally produce sobriety and frugality, if judiciously imposed: and being confounded

* See Sketches of the History of Man, page 474, & seq.

with

with the natural price of the commodity, they are ſcarcely perceived by the conſumers.—Their only diſadvantage is, that they are expenſive in the levying.—Another thing is, a duty upon commodities checks itſelf; and a miniſter will ſoon find, that an increaſe of the impoſt is no increaſe of the revenue. It is not eaſy, therefore, for a people to be altogether ruined by ſuch taxes.

Taxes upon *poſſeſſions* are levied without expence; but have every other diſadvantage.—Moſt ſtates, however, are obliged to have recourſe to them, in order to ſupply the deficiencies of the other.

As *taxes* take nothing out of a country; as they do not diminiſh the public ſtock, only vary the diſtribution of it, they are not *neceſſarily* prejudicial to happineſs.—If the ſtate exact money from certain members of the community, ſhe diſpenſes it alſo amongſt other members of the ſame community.—They who contribute to the revenue, and they who are ſupported or benefited by the expences of government, are to be placed one againſt the other; and, whilſt what the ſubſiſtence of one part is profited by receiving, compenſates for what that of the other ſuffers by paying, the common fund of the ſociety is not leſſened.—This is true: but it muſt be obſerved, that although the ſum diſtributed by the ſtate be always EQUAL to the ſum collected from the people, yet the gain and loſſes to the means of ſubſiſtence may be very UNEQUAL; and *the balance will remain on the wrong or the right ſide of the account, according as the money paſſes by taxation from the induſtrious to the idle, from the many to the few, from thoſe who want to thoſe who abound, or in a contrary direction.*

For inſtance, a tax upon *coaches*, to be laid out in the repair of *roads*, would probably *improve* the happineſs of a neighbourhood; a tax upon *cottages*, to be ultimately expended in the purchaſe and ſupport of *coaches*, would certainly *diminiſh* it.

In like manner, a tax upon *wine* or *tea*, diſtributed in bounties to *fiſhermen* or *huſbandmen*, would *augment* the proviſion of a country; a tax upon *fiſheries* and *huſbandry*, however indirect or concealed, to be converted, when raiſed, to the procuring of *wine* or *tea* for the idle and opulent, would naturally *impair* the public ſtock.

The EFFECT, therefore, of *taxes* upon the means of ſubſiſtence depends not ſo much upon the amount of the ſum levied, as upon the *object* of the tax, and *the application.*

Taxes

Taxes likewise may be so adjusted as to conduce to the restraint of *luxury*, and the *correction* of *vice** ; to the encouragement

* When the expediency of laying a further tax on distillation of spirituous liquors was canvassed before the House of Commons some years ago, it was said of the distillers with great truth, " *They take the bread from the people, and convert it into poison.*" Yet is this manufacture of disease permitted to continue, as appears by its paying into the treasury above 900,000 l. near a million of money annually.

It is generally allowed, " *that government is for the benefit of the governed and not the governors,*" and no deviation should exist to this fundamental principle. *Get money*, was the advice of a father to his son,—honestly if you can,—if not,—*Get money*. It is also a question, How far the king's patent to quack remedies is expedient, as it discourages an useful body of men, favours imposition, begets incredulity, and is the destruction of the lives and the health of thousands. *Get money* can never be an excuse in a free government, where *happiness in the subject* is its avowed principle.

MONOPOLIES and CHARTERS.—*James* the First granted many of these, and his *son* followed his example. Between them *both* almost every trade was confined in a few hands; but these *monopolists* paid heavy sums for becoming the *elder children* of a *partial father*. *Monopolies* had crept in during the reign of Queen ELIZABETH; but that great queen, finding that the House of Commons was uneasy, called in most of these grants. The House of Commons, struck with this generosity of the queen, in meeting their desires, and anticipating their requests, deputed one hundred and forty of their members to wait upon her with their thanks. To their address the queen returned an answer, which, as flowing from her heart, made the deepest impression on her subjects. —I shall subjoin a part:

" GENTLEMEN,

" I owe you hearty thanks and commendations, for your singular good will towards me, not only in your heart and thoughts, but which you have openly expressed and declared, whereby you have recalled me from an error proceeding from my *ignorance*, not my *will*. These things had undeservedly turned *encouragement* of *industry*, *trade*, *agriculture*, and *marriage*. —Taxes thus contrived become *rewards* and *penalties*; not only SOURCES OF REVENUE, but INSTRUMENTS OF POLICE.—Vices indeed themselves cannot be taxed without holding forth such a conditional toleration of them as to destroy men's perception of their guilt: a tax comes in time to be considered as a commutation: the materials, however, and incentives of vice may.—Although, for instance, drunkenness would be, on this account, an unfit object of taxation, yet public-houses and spirituous liquors are very properly subject to heavy imposts.

Nevertheless, although it may be true, that taxes cannot be pronounced to be detrimental to happiness, by any absolute necessity in their nature; and though, un-

turned to my disgrace (to whom nothing is more dear than the safety and love of my people), had not such harpies and horse-leeches as these been discovered to me by you. I HAD RATHER MY HEART OR HAND SHOULD PERISH, THAN THAT EITHER MY HEART OR HAND SHOULD ALLOW SUCH PRIVILEGES TO MONOPOLISTS, AS MAY BE PREJUDICIAL TO THE BODY OF MY PEOPLE. The splendour of regal majesty hath not so blinded mine eyes, that LICENTIOUS POWER should prevail with me more than JUSTICE. *I know that the commonwealth is to be governed for the good and advantage of* THOSE *that are committed to me, not of* MYSELF, *to whom it is intrusted; and that an account is one day to be given before another judgment seat.* I think myself most happy, that, by GOD's assistance, I have hitherto so prosperously governed the commonwealth in all respects; and that I have *such subjects*, as for their good I would willingly leave both my kingdom and my life." &c. &c.

der

der ſome modifications, and when urged only to a certain extent, they may even operate in favour of it; yet it will be found, *in a great plurality of inſtances*, that their tendency is noxious.—*Let it be ſuppoſed that nine families inhabit a neighbourhood, each poſſeſſing barely the means of ſubſiſtence, or of that mode of ſubſiſtence which cuſtom hath eſtabliſhed amongſt them; let a tenth family be quartered upon theſe, to be ſupported by a tax raiſed from the nine; or rather let one of the nine have his income augmented by a ſimilar deduction from the incomes of the reſt: in either of theſe caſes, it is evident that the whole diſtrict would be broken up.*—For as the *entire income* of each is ſuppoſed to be *barely ſufficient* for the eſtabliſhment which it maintains, a *deduction* of *any part* deſtroys *that eſtabliſhment*.—Now it is no anſwer to this objection, it is no apology for the grievance, to ſay, "*that nothing is taken out of the neighbourhood; that the ſtock is not diminiſhed.*"—The miſchief is done by *deranging* the *diſtribution*.—Nor, again, is the luxury of *one* family, or even the maintenance of an additional family, a recompenſe to the country for the ruin of *nine* others.—Nor, laſtly, will it alter the effect, though it may conceal the cauſe, that the diſtribution, inſtead of being levied directly upon

 each

each day's wages, is mixed up in the price of ſome article of conſtant uſe and conſumption ; as in a tax upon candles, malt, leather, or fuel.

It ſeems neceſſary, however, to diſtinguiſh between the operation of a *new tax*, and the effect of taxes which have been long eſtabliſhed.—In the courſe of circulation the money may flow back to the hands from which it was taken.—The proportion between the ſupply and the expence of ſubſiſtence, which had been diſturbed by the tax, may at length recover itſelf again.—In the inſtance juſt now ſtated, the addition of a tenth family to the neighbourhood, or the enlarged expences of one of the nine, may, in ſome ſhape or other, ſo advance the profits, or increaſe the employment of the reſt, as to make full reſtitution for the ſhare of their property, of which it deprives them: or, what is more likely to happen, a reduction may take place in their mode of living, ſuited to the abridgment of their incomes.—*Yet ſtill the ultimate and permanent effect of taxation, though diſtinguiſhable from the impreſſion of a new tax, is generally adverſe to induſtry.*—The *proportion* above ſpoken of, can only be reſtored by one ſide or other of the following alternative; *by the people either* CONTRACTING THEIR WANTS,

which

which at the ſame time diminiſhes conſumption and employment; *or by* RAISING THE PRICE OF LABOUR, *which neceſſarily adding to the price of the productions and manufactures of the country, checks their ſale at foreign markets.*

A nation which is *burthened* with *taxes*, muſt always be *underſold* by a nation which is *free* from them, unleſs the difference be made up by ſome ſingular advantage of climate, ſoil, ſkill, or induſtry.—*This quality belongs to all taxes which affect the maſs of the community, even when impoſed upon the propereſt objects, and applied to the faireſt purpoſes.*—BUT ABUSES ARE INSEPARABLE FROM THE DISPOSAL OF PUBLIC MONEY.—AS GOVERNMENTS ARE USUALLY ADMINISTERED, THE PRODUCE OF PUBLIC TAXES IS EXPENDED UPON A TRAIN OF GENTRY, IN THE MAINTAINING OF POMP, OR IN THE PURCHASE OF INFLUENCE.—The converſion of property, which *taxes* effectuate, when they are employed in this manner, is attended with *obvious evils.*—IT TAKES FROM THE INDUSTRIOUS TO GIVE TO THE IDLE; IT INCREASES THE NUMBER OF THE LATTER; IT TENDS TO ACCUMULATION; IT SACRIFICES THE CONVENIENCY OF MANY TO THE LUXURY OF A FEW; IT MAKES NO RETURN TO THE PEOPLE, FROM WHOM

THE TAX IS DRAWN, THAT IS SATISFACTORY OR INTELLIGIBLE; IT ENCOURAGES NO ACTIVITY WHICH IS USEFUL OR PRODUCTIVE.

The ſum to be raiſed being ſettled, a *wiſe ſtateſman* will contrive his taxes principally with a view to their effect upon general happineſs, that is, he will ſo adjuſt them, as to give the leaſt poſſible obſtruction to thoſe means of ſubſiſtence by which the maſs of the community are maintained.—We are accuſtomed to an opinion "*that a tax, to be juſt, ought to be accurately proportioned to the circumſtances of the perſons who pay it.*"—The point to be regarded, IS NOT WHAT MEN HAVE, BUT WHAT THEY CAN SPARE; and it is evident that a man who poſſeſſes a *thouſand pounds* a year can more eaſily give up a *hundred*, than a man with a *hundred pounds* a year can part with *ten*; that is, *thoſe habits of life* which are *reaſonable* and *innocent*, and upon the ability to continue which the formation of families depends, will be much leſs affected by the one deduction than the other: it is ſtill more evident, that a man of a hundred pounds a year would not be ſo much diſtreſſed in his ſubſiſtence by a demand from him of ten pounds, as a man of ten pounds a year would be by the loſs of one: to which we muſt add, that

the

the population of every country being replenifhed by the marriages of the *loweft ranks* of the fociety, *their accommodation* and *relief* becomes of *more importance* to the ftate, than *the conveniency* of any *higher* but *lefs numerous order* of its citizens.—But whatever be the proportion which public expediency directs, whether the fimple, the duplicate, or any higher or intermediate proportion of men's incomes, it can never be attained by any fingle tax; as no fingle object of taxation can be found, which meafures the ability of the fubject with fufficient generality and exactnefs.—It is only by a fyftem and variety of taxes mutually balancing and equalizing one another, that a due proportion can be preferved.—For inftance, if a tax upon lands prefs with greater hardfhip upon thofe who live in the country, it may be properly counterpoifed by a tax upon the rent of houfes, which will affect principally the inhabitants of large towns.—Diftinctions may alfo be framed in fome taxes, which fhall allow abatements or exemptions to married perfons; to the parents of a certain number of legitimate children; to the education of youth; to improvers of the foil; to particular modes of cultivation, as to tillage in preference to pafturage; and in general to that induſtry which is immediately *productive*, in preference to that which is only *inſtrumental*; but above all, which may leave the heavieſt part of the burthen upon the methods, whatever they be, of acquiring wealth without induſtry, or even of ſubſiſting in idleneſs*.

* PALEY.

SECT.

SECT. VIII.

ON THE ADVANTAGES OF SOCIETY, AND THE DISTRIBUTION OF LABOUR.

Do you think, that without ſociety you or any man could have been born?—Without ſociety, when born, could you have been brought to maturity?—Had your parents then had no ſocial affections towards you in that perilous ſtate, that tedious infancy (ſo much longer than the longeſt of other animals), you muſt have inevitably periſhed through want and inability.—You perceive then that to ſociety you and every man are indebted, not only for the beginning of being, but for the continuance.

Suppoſe then we paſs from this birth and infancy of man, to his maturity and perfection.——Is there any age, think you, ſo ſelf-ſufficient as that in it he feels no wants?—In the firſt and principal place that of food; then perhaps that of raiment; and after this, a dwelling or defence againſt the weather.—Theſe wants are ſurely natural at all ages.—And is it not agreeable to nature that they ſhould at all ages be ſupplied?—And is it not more agreeable to have them well ſupplied, than ill?—And moſt agreeable to have them beſt ſupplied?—If there be then any one ſtate better than all others for the ſupplying theſe wants, this ſtate of all others muſt needs be moſt natural.

And what ſupply of theſe wants ſhall we eſteem the meaneſt which we can conceive?—Would it not be ſomething like this? Nothing beyond acorns for food, beyond a rude ſkin for raiment, or beyond a cavern or hollow tree to provide us with a dwelling?—Indeed this would be bad enough.—And do you not imagine, as far as this, we might each ſupply ourſelves, though we lived in woods, mere ſolitary ſavages?

Suppoſe then that our ſupplies were to be mended—for inſtance, that we were to exchange acorns for bread.—Would our *ſaving character* be ſufficient here?—Muſt we not be a little better diſciplined?—Would not ſome art be requiſite?—The baker's, for example.—And previouſly to the baker's, that of the miller?—And previouſly to the miller's, that of the huſbandman?—Three

arts

arts then appear neceſſary, even upon the loweſt eſtimation.

But a queſtion farther—Can the huſbandman work, think you, without his tools?—Muſt he not have his plough, his harrow, his reap-hook, and the like?—And muſt not thoſe other artiſts too be furniſhed in the ſame manner?—And whence muſt they be furniſhed? From their own arts.—Or are not the making tools, and the uſing them, two different occupations?—Does agriculture make its own plough, its own harrow?—Or does it not apply to other arts for all neceſſaries of this kind?—Again—Does the baker build his own oven, or the miller frame his own mill?

What a tribe of mechanics then are advancing upon us?—Smiths, carpenters, maſons, mill-wrights—and all theſe to provide the ſingle neceſſary of bread.—Not leſs than ſeven or eight arts, we find, are wanting at the feweſt.—And what if, to the providing a comfortable cottage, and raiment ſuitable to an induſtrious hind, we allow a dozen arts more?—It would be eaſy, by the ſame reaſoning, to prove the number double.

If ſo it ſhould ſeem, that towards a tolerable ſupply of the three primary and common neceſſaries, FOOD, RAI-

MENT,

MENT, and a DWELLING, not leſs than twenty arts were, on the loweſt account, requiſite.

And is one man equal, think you, to the exerciſe of theſe twenty arts?—If he had even genius, which we can ſcarce imagine, is it poſſible he ſhould find leiſure?—If ſo, then a ſolitary unſocial ſtate can never ſupply tolerably the common neceſſaries of life.

But what if we paſs from the *neceſſaries* of life to the *elegancies?*—To muſic, ſculpture, painting, and poetry?—What if we paſs from all arts, whether neceſſary or elegant, to the large and various tribe of Sciences? To logic, mathematics, aſtronomy, phyſics?—Can one man, imagine you, maſter all this?—And yet in this cycle of ſciences and arts ſeem included the comforts as well as ornaments of life.

What then muſt be done? In what manner muſt we be ſupplied?—I know not how, unleſs we make a diſtribution.—Let one exerciſe one art, and another a different—let this man ſtudy ſuch a ſcience, and that man another.—Thus the whole cycle may be carried eaſily into perfection.

Now we ſee a new face of things.—The *ſavages*, with their ſkins and their caverns, diſappear.—In their place I behold a fair community riſing.—No longer woods, no longer ſolitude; but all is ſocial, civil, and cultivated. —And can we doubt any farther whether ſociety be natural?—Is not this evidently the ſtate which can beſt ſupply the primary wants?—And did we not agree ſome time ſince, that this ſtate, whatever we found it, would be certainly of all others the moſt agreeable to our nature?—We did.—And have we not added, ſince this, to the weight of our argument, by paſſing from the neceſſary arts to the elegant; from the elegant to the ſciences? We have.—The more we conſider, the more ſhall we be convinced, that all theſe, the nobleſt honours and ornaments of the human mind, without that leiſure, that experience, that emulation, that reward, which the *ſocial ſtate* alone we know is able to provide them, could never have found exiſtence, or been in the leaſt recognized.

LET IT NOT BE FORGOTTEN THEN, IN FAVOUR OF SOCIETY, THAT TO IT WE OWE, NOT ONLY THE BEGINNING AND CONTINUATION, BUT THE WELL-BEING, AND (IF I MAY USE THE EXPRESSION) THE VERY ELEGANCE AND RATIONALITY OF OUR EXISTENCE.

And what then, if ſociety be thus agreeable to our nature, is there nothing, think you, within us to excite and lead us to it? No impulse, no preparation of faculties?—It would be ſtrange if there ſhould not.—It would be a ſingular exception with reſpect to all other herding ſpecies.—Let us however examine—*pity, benevolence, friendſhip, love*; *the general diſlike of ſolitude, and deſire of company*; are they natural affections which come of themſelves; or are they taught us by art, like muſic and arithmetic?—And are not the powers and capacities of ſpeech the ſame? Are not all men naturally formed to expreſs their ſentiments by ſome kind of language?

If then theſe ſeveral powers and diſpoſitions are natural, ſo ſhould ſeem too their exerciſe.—And if their exerciſe, then ſo too that ſtate where alone they can be exerciſed.—And what is this ſtate but the ſocial?—Or where elſe is it poſſible to converſe, or uſe our ſpeech; to exhibit actions of *pity*, *benevolence*, *friendſhip*, or *love*; to relieve our averſion to ſolitude, or gratify our deſire of being with others?

You ſee then a preparation of faculties is not wanting. We are fitted with *powers* and *diſpoſitions* which have only *relation* to ſociety; and which, out of ſociety, can no where elſe be exerciſed.—You have ſeen, too,

the

the ſuperior advantages of the ſocial ſtate above all others.

LET THIS THEN EVER BE REMEMBERED, REMEMBERED AS A FIRST PRINCIPLE IN OUR IDEAS OF HUMANITY, THAT MAN BY NATURE IS TRULY A SOCIAL ANIMAL *.

The effects of *the diviſion of labour*, in the general buſineſs of ſociety, will be more eaſily underſtood by conſidering in what manner it operates in ſome particular manufactures.—It is commonly ſuppoſed to be carried fartheſt in ſome very *trifling* ones; not perhaps that it really is carried further in them than in others of more *importance*: but in thoſe trifling manufactures which are deſtined to ſupply the ſmall wants of but a ſmall number of people, the whole number of workmen muſt neceſſarily be ſmall; and thoſe employed in every different branch of the work can often be collected into the ſame workhouſe, and placed at once under the view of the ſpectator.—In thoſe *great manufactures*, on the contrary, which are deſtined to ſupply the great wants of the great body of the people, every different branch of the work employs ſo great a number of workmen,

* *Harris*.

that it is impoſſible to collect them all into the ſame workhouſe.—We can ſeldom ſee more, at one time, than thoſe employed in one ſingle branch.—Though in ſuch manufactures, therefore, the work may really be divided into a much greater number of parts than in thoſe of a more trifling nature, the diviſion is not near ſo obvious, and has accordingly been much leſs obſerved.

But to take an example from a very trifling manufacture; but one in which the diviſion of labour has been very often taken notice of, the trade of the *pin-maker*; a workman not educated to this buſineſs (which the diviſion of labour has rendered a diſtinct trade), nor acquainted with the uſe of the machinery employed in it (to the invention of which the ſame diviſion of labour has probably given occaſion), could ſcarce, perhaps, with his utmoſt induſtry, make *one* pin in a day, and certainly could not *twenty*.—But in the way in which this buſineſs is now carried on, not only the whole work is a peculiar trade, but it is divided into a number of branches, of which the greater part are likewiſe peculiar trades.—*One man draws out the wire, another ſtraights it, a third cuts it, a fourth points it, a fifth grinds it at the top for receiving the head; to make the head requires two or three diſtinct operations; to put it*

on

on is a peculiar bufinefs, to whiten the pins is another; it is even a trade by itfelf to put them into the paper; and the important bufinefs of making a pin is, in this manner, divided into about *eighteen* diftinct operations, which, in fome manufactories, are all performed by diftinct hands, though in others the fame man will fometimes perform two or three of them.—I have feen a fmall manufactory of this kind where ten men only were employed, and where fome of them confequently performed two or three diftinct operations.—But though they were very poor, and therefore but indifferently accommodated with the neceffary machinery, they could, when they exerted themfelves, make among them about *twelve pounds of pins in a day*.—There are in a pound upwards of *four thoufand* pins of a middling fize.—Thofe ten perfons, therefore, could make among them upwards of *forty-eight thoufand* pins in a day.—Each perfon, therefore, making a tenth part of forty-eight thoufand pins, might be confidered as making *four thoufand eight hundred* pins in a day.—But if they had all wrought feparately and independently, and without any of them having been educated to this peculiar bufinefs, they certainly could not each of them have made *twenty*, perhaps not *one* pin in a day; that is, certainly, not the two

hundred

hundred and fortieth, perhaps not the four thousand eight hundredth part of what they are at present capable of performing, IN CONSEQUENCE *of a proper division and combination of their different operations.*

In every other art and manufacture, the effects of *the division of labour* are similar to what they are in this very trifling one; though in many of them the labour can neither be so much subdivided, nor reduced to so great a simplicity of operation.—The division of labour, however, so far as it can be introduced, occasions in every art a proportionable increase of the productive powers of labour.—The separation of different trades and employments from one another, seems to have taken place in consequence of this advantage.—This separation too is generally carried furthest in those countries which enjoy the highest degree of industry and improvement; what is the work of one man in a rude state of society being generally that of several in an improved one.—In every improved society the farmer is generally nothing but a farmer, the manufacturer nothing but a manufacturer. —The labour too which is necessary to produce any one complete manufacture, is almost always divided among a great number of hands.—How many different trades are employed in each branch of the linen and woollen manufactures, from the growers of the flax and the wool to the bleachers and ſmoothers of the linen, or to the dyers and dreſſers of the cloth!

The great increaſe in the quantity of work which, IN CONSEQUENCE of *the diviſion of labour*, the ſame number of people are capable of performing, is owing to *three* different circumſtances.

1. To the increaſe of *dexterity* in every particular workman.

2. To the *ſaving of* the *time* which is commonly loſt in paſſing from one ſpecies of work to another.

And 3. To the invention of a great number of *machines* which facilitate and abridge labour, and enable one man to do the work of many.

FIRST, the improvement of the *dexterity* of the workman neceſſarily increaſes the quantity of the work he can perform; and the diviſion of labour, by reducing every man's buſineſs to ſome one ſimple operation, and by making this operation the ſole employment of his life, neceſſarily increaſes very much the dexterity of the workman.

A *common ſmith*, who, though accuſtomed to handle the hammer, has never been uſed to make nails, if upon ſome particular occaſion he is obliged to attempt it, will

will ſcarce, I am aſſured, be able to make above *two* or *three hundred* ***nails*** in a day, and thoſe too very bad ones.

A *ſmith* who has been accuſtomed to make nails, but whoſe ſole or principal buſineſs has not been that of a nailer, can ſeldom with his utmoſt diligence make more than *eight hundred* or a *thouſand nails* in a day.

I have ſeen ſeveral boys under twenty years of age who had never exerciſed any other trade but that of making nails, and who, when they exerted themſelves, could make each of them upwards of two thouſand three hundred nails in a day.

The making of a nail, however, is by no means one of the ſimpleſt operations.—The ſame perſon blows the bellows, ſtirs or mends the fire as there is occaſion, heats the iron, and forges every part of the nail: in forging the head too he is obliged to change his tools.—The different operations into which the making of a pin, or of a metal button, is ſubdivided, are all of them much more ſimple, and the dexterity of the perſon, of whoſe life it has been the ſole buſineſs to perform them, is uſually much greater.—The rapidity with which ſome of the operations of thoſe manufactures are performed, exceeds

ceeds what the human hand could, by thofe who had never feen them, be fuppofed capable of acquiring.

Secondly, the advantage which is gained *by faving the time commonly loft in paffing from one fort of work to another*, is much greater than we fhould at firft view be apt to imagine it.—It is impoffible to pafs very quickly from one kind of work to another, that is carried on in a different place, and with quite different tools.—A country weaver, who cultivates a fmall farm, muft lofe a good deal of time in paffing from his loom to the field, and from the field to his loom.—When the two trades can be carried on in the fame workhoufe, the lofs of time is, no doubt, much lefs.—It is even in this cafe, however, very confiderable.—A man commonly faunters a little in turning his hand from one fort of employment to another.—When he firft begins the new work he is feldom very keen and hearty; his mind, as they fay, does not go to it, and for fome time he rather trifles than applies to good purpofe.—The habit of fauntering, and of indolent carelefs application, which is naturally, or rather neceffarily, acquired by every country workman who is obliged to change his work and his tools every half hour, and to apply his hand in twenty different ways almost every day of his life; renders him almost always slothful and lazy, and incapable of any vigorous application even on the most pressing occasions.—Independent, therefore, of his deficiency in point of dexterity, *this cause alone* must always reduce considerably the quantity of work which he is capable of performing.

THIRDLY, and lastly, every body must be sensible how much labour is facilitated and abridged by the application of proper *machinery.*—It is unnecessary to give any example.—I shall only observe, therefore, that the invention of all those machines by which labour is so much facilitated and abridged, seems to have been originally owing to the division of labour *.—Men are much

* A *broad-wheeled waggon,* attended by two men, and drawn by eight horses, in about six weeks time carries and brings back between London and Edinburgh near four ton weight of goods. In about the same time a ship, navigated by six or eight men, and sailing between the ports of London and Leith, frequently carries and brings back two hundred ton weight of goods. *Six or eight* men, therefore, by the help of WATER-CARRIAGE, can carry and bring back in the same time the same quantity of goods between London and Edinburgh, as *fifty broad-wheeled waggons,* attended by a *hundred men,* and drawn by *four hundred horses.* Upon two hundred tons of goods, therefore, carried by the cheapest land-carriage from London to Edinburgh, there must be charged the maintenance of a hundred men for three weeks, and both the maintenance, and, what is nearly equal to the maintenance, the wear and tear of four hundred horses as well as of fifty great waggons. *Whereas, upon the same quantity of goods carried by water, there is to be charged only the maintenance*

much more likely to difcover eafier and readier methods of attaining any object, when the whole attention of their minds is directed towards that fingle object, than when it is diffipated among a great variety of things.—But in confequence of the divifion of labour, the whole of every man's attention comes naturally to be directed towards fome one very fimple object.—It is naturally to be expected, therefore, that fome one or other of thofe who are employed in each particular branch of labour fhould foon find out eafier and readier methods of performing their own particular work, wherever the nature of it admits of fuch improvement.—A great part of

tenance of fix or eight men, and the wear and tear of a fhip of two hundred tons burthen, together with the value of the fuperior rifk, or the difference of the infurance between land and water-carriage. Were there no other communication between thofe two places, therefore, but by land-carriage, as no goods could be tranfported from the one to the other, except fuch whofe price was very confiderable in proportion to their weight, they could carry on but a fmall part of that commerce which at prefent fubfifts between them, and confequently could give but a fmall part of that encouragement which they at prefent mutually afford to each other's induftry. There could be little or no commerce of any kind between the diftant parts of the world. What goods could bear the expence of land-carriage between London and Calcutta? Or if there were any fo precious as to be able to fupport this expence, with what fafety could they be tranfported through the territories of fo many barbarous nations? Thofe two cities, however, at prefent carry on a very confiderable commerce with each other, and by mutually affording a market, give a good deal of encouragement to each other's induftry.

the machines made uſe of in thoſe manufactures in which labour is moſt ſubdivided, were originally the inventions of common workmen, who, being each of them employed in ſome very ſimple operation, naturally turned their thoughts towards finding out eaſier and readier methods of performing it.—Whoever has been much accuſtomed to viſit ſuch manufactures, muſt frequently have been ſhewn very pretty machines which were the inventions of ſuch workmen, in order to facilitate and quicken their own particular part of the work. —*In the firſt fire-engines a boy was conſtantly employed to open and ſhut alternately the communication between the boiler and the cylinder, according as the piſton either aſcended or deſcended.—One of thoſe boys, who loved to play with his companions, obſerved that, by tying a ſtring from the handle of the valve which opened this communication to another part of the machine, the valve would open and ſhut without his aſſiſtance, and leave him at liberty to divert himſelf with his play-fellows.*—One of the greateſt improvements that has been made upon this machine ſince it was firſt invented, was in this manner the diſcovery of a *boy* who wanted to ſave his own labour.

All the improvements in machinery, however, have by no means been the inventions of thoſe who had oc-

 caſion

caſion to uſe the machines.—Many improvements have been made by the ingenuity of the makers of the machines, when to make them became the buſineſs of a peculiar trade; and ſome by that of thoſe who are called philoſophers, or men of ſpeculation, whoſe trade it is not to do any thing, but to obſerve every thing; and who, upon that account, are often capable of *combining* together the powers of the moſt diſtant and diſſimilar objects.—In the progreſs of ſociety, *philoſophy* or *ſpeculation* becomes, like every other employment, the principal or ſole occupation of a particular claſs of citizens.—Like every other employment too, it is ſubdivided into a great number of different branches, each of which affords occupation to a peculiar tribe or claſs of philoſophers; and this ſubdiviſion of employment in philoſophy, as well as in every other buſineſs, improves dexterity, and ſaves time.—Each individual becomes more expert in his own peculiar branch, more work is done upon the whole, and the quantity of ſcience is conſiderably increaſed by it.

IT IS THE GREAT MULTIPLICATION OF THE PRODUCTIONS OF ALL THE DIFFERENT ARTS, IN CONSEQUENCE OF THE DIVISION OF LABOUR, WHICH OCCASIONS, IN A WELL-GOVERNED SOCIETY, THAT UNIVERSAL

VERSAL OPULENCE WHICH EXTENDS ITSELF TO THE LOWEST RANKS OF THE PEOPLE.—EVERY WORKMAN HAS A GREAT QUANTITY OF HIS OWN WORK TO DISPOSE OF BEYOND WHAT HE HIMSELF HAS OCCASION FOR; AND EVERY OTHER WORKMAN BEING EXACTLY IN THE SAME SITUATION, HE IS ENABLED TO EXCHANGE A GREAT QUANTITY OF HIS OWN GOODS FOR A GREAT QUANTITY, OR, WHAT COMES TO THE SAME THING, FOR THE PRICE OF A GREAT QUANTITY OF THEIRS.—HE SUPPLIES THEM ABUNDANTLY WITH WHAT THEY HAVE OCCASION FOR, AND THEY ACCOMMODATE HIM AS AMPLY WITH WHAT HE HAS OCCASION FOR, AND A GENERAL PLENTY DIFFUSES ITSELF THROUGH ALL THE DIFFERENT RANKS OF THE SOCIETY.

Obferve the *accommodation* of the moft common artificer or day-labourer in a civilized and thriving country, and you will perceive that the number of people of whofe induftry a part, though but a fmall part, has been employed in procuring him this accommodation, exceeds all computation.—*The woollen coat, for example, which covers the day-labourer, as coarfe and rough as it may appear, is the produce of the joint labour of a great multitude of workmen.—The fhepherd, the forter of the wool, the wool-*

*wool-comber or carder, the dyer, the scribbler, the spinner, the weaver, the fuller, the dresser, with many others, must all join their different arts in order to complete even this homely production**.—*How many merchants and carriers, besides, must have been employed in transporting the materials from some of those workmen to others, who often live in a very distant part of the country! how much commerce and navigation in particular; how many ship-builders, sailors, sail-makers, rope-makers, must have been employed in order to bring together the different drugs made use of by the dyer, which often come from the remotest corners of the world! What a variety of labour too is necessary in order to produce the tools of the meanest of those workmen! To say nothing of such complicated machines as the ship of the sailor, the mill of the fuller, or even the loom of the weaver, let us consider only what a variety of labour is requisite in order to form that very simple machine, the shears with which the shepherd*

* In civilized society man stands at all times in need of the co-operation and assistance of *great multitudes*, while his *whole life* is scarce *sufficient* to gain the *friendship* of a *few persons*. In almost every other race of animals, each individual, when it is grown up to maturity, is entirely independent, and in its natural state has occasion for the assistance of no other living creature. But man has almost constant occasion for the help of his brethren, and it is in vain for him to expect it from their *benevolence* only. He will be more likely to prevail if he can interest their *self-love* in his favour, and shew them that it is for their own advantage to do for him what he requires of them.—*Vide the Sect. on the Principle of Trade.*

clips

clips the wool.—The miner, the builder of the furnace for ſmelting the ore, the feller of the timber, the burner of the charcoal to be made uſe of in the ſmelting-houſe, the brick-maker, the brick-layer, the workmen who attend the furnace, the mill-wright, the forger, the ſmith, muſt all of them join their different arts in order to produce them.—Were we to examine, in the ſame manner, all the different parts of his *dreſs* and *houſehold furniture*, the *coarſe linen ſhirt* which he wears next his ſkin, the *ſhoes* which cover his feet, the *bed* which he lies on, and all the different parts which compoſe it, the *kitchen-grate* at which he prepares his victuals, the *coals* which he makes uſe of for that purpoſe, dug from the bowels of the earth, and brought to him perhaps by a long ſea and a long land carriage, all the other *utenſils* of his kitchen, all the *furniture* of his table, the *knives* and *forks*, the *earthen* or *pewter plates* upon which he ſerves up and divides his victuals, the different hands employed in preparing his *bread* and his *beer*, the *glaſs window* which lets in the heat and the light, and keeps out the wind and the rain, with all the knowledge and art requiſite for preparing that beautiful and happy invention, without which theſe northern parts of the world could ſcarce have afforded a very comfortable habitation, together with the *tools* of all the different

workmen

workmen employed in producing thoſe different conveniencies; if we examine, I ſay, all theſe things, and conſider what a variety of labour is employed about each of them, we ſhall be ſenſible that *without* the aſſiſtance and *co-operation* of *many thouſands*, the very *meaneſt perſon* in a *civilized country* could not be provided, even according to, what we very falſely imagine, the eaſy and ſimple manner in which he is commonly accommodated.—Compared, indeed, with the more extravagant luxury of the great, his accommodation muſt no doubt appear extremely ſimple and eaſy; and yet it may be true, perhaps, that the accommodation of an European prince does not always ſo much exceed that of an induſtrious and frugal peaſant, as the accommodation of the latter exceeds that of many *an African king*, the abſolute maſter of the lives and liberties of ten thouſand naked ſavages*.

* Adam Smith.

SECT. IX.

ON THE INTRODUCTION OF MONEY.

When *the division of labour* has been once thoroughly eſtabliſhed, it is but a very ſmall part of a man's wants which the produce of his own labour can ſupply.—He ſupplies the far greater part of them by exchanging that ſurplus part of the produce of his own labour, which is over and above his own conſumption, for ſuch parts of the produce of other men's labour as he has occaſion for. —Every man thus lives by *exchanging*, or becomes in ſome meaſure a merchant, and the ſociety itſelf grows to be what is properly a commercial ſociety.

But when the diviſion of labour *firſt* began to take place, this power of exchanging muſt frequently have been very much clogged and embarraſſed in its operations.—One man, we ſhall ſuppoſe, has more of a certain commodity than he himſelf has occaſion for, while another has leſs.—The former conſequently would be

glad

glad to difpofe of, and the latter to purchafe, a part of this fuperfluity.—But if this latter fhould chance to have nothing that the former ftands in need of, no exchange can be made between them.—The butcher has more meat in his fhop than he himfelf can confume, and the brewer and the baker would each of them be willing to purchafe a part of it.—But they have nothing to offer in exchange, except the different productions of their refpective trades, and the butcher is already provided with all the bread and beer which he has immediate occafion for.—No exchange can, in this cafe, be made between them.—He cannot be their merchant, nor they his cuftomers; and they are all of them thus mutually lefs ferviceable to one another.—*In order to remove the inconveniency of fuch fituations,* every prudent man in every period of fociety, after the firft eftablifhment of the divifion of labour, muft naturally have endeavoured to manage his affairs in fuch a manner, as to have at all times by him, befides the peculiar produce of his own induftry, a certain quantity of fome one commodity or other, fuch as he imagined few people would be likely to refufe in exchange for the produce of their induftry.

Many different commodities, it is probable, were fucceffively both thought of and employed for this purpofe. —In the rude ages of fociety, cattle are faid to have been the common inftrument of commerce; and, though they muft have been a moft inconvenient one, yet in old times we find things were frequently valued according to the number of cattle which had been given in exchange for them.—The armour of Diomede, fays Homer, coft only *nine oxen*; but that of Glaucus coft *an hundred oxen*.—*Salt* is faid to be the common inftrument of commerce and exchanges in ABYSSINIA; a fpecies of *fhells* in fome parts of the COAST of INDIA; dried *cod* at NEWFOUNDLAND; *tobacco* in VIRGINIA; *fugar* in fome of our WEST INDIA COLONIES; *hides* or *dreffed leather* in fome other countries; and there is at this day a village in SCOTLAND where it is not uncommon, I am told, for a workman to carry *nails* inftead of money to the baker's fhop or the ale-houfe.

In all countries, however, men feem at laft to have been determined by irrefiftible reafons to give the preference, for this employment, to metals above every other commodity.—Metals can not only be kept with as little lofs as any other commodity, fcarce any thing being lefs perifhable than they are, but they can likewife, without any lofs, be divided into any number of parts, as by fufion thofe

parts

parts can eaſily be reunited again; a quality which no other equally durable commodities poſſeſs, and which more than any other quality renders them fit to be the inſtruments of commerce and circulation.—The man who wanted to buy ſalt, for example, and had nothing but cattle to give in exchange for it, muſt have been obliged to buy ſalt to the value of a whole ox, or a whole ſheep, at a time.—He could ſeldom buy leſs than this, becauſe what he was to give for it could ſeldom be divided without loſs; and if he had a mind to buy more, he muſt, for the ſame reaſons, have been obliged to buy double or triple the quantity, the value, to wit, of two or three oxen, or of two or three ſheep.—If, on the contrary, inſtead of ſheep or oxen, he had *metals* to give in exchange for it, he could eaſily *proportion* the quantity of the metal to the precise quantity of the commodity which he had immediate occaſion for*.

It is in this manner that money has become in all civilized nations the universal instrument of commerce, by the intervention of which goods of all kinds are bought and sold, or exchanged for one another.

* Adam Smith.

SECT.

SECT. X.

OF THE PRICE OF COMMODITIES.

In that early and rude ſtate of ſociety which precedes both the accumulation of ſtock and the appropriation of land, the proportion between the quantities of labour neceſſary for acquiring different objects ſeems to be the only circumſtance which can afford any rule for exchanging them for one another.—If among a nation of hunters, for example, *it uſually coſts twice the labour* to kill a beaver which it does to kill a deer, *one beaver* ſhould naturally exchange for, or be worth *two deer*.—It is natural that what is uſually the produce of two days or two hours labour, ſhould be worth double of what is uſually the produce of one day's or one hour's labour.

If the one ſpecies of labour ſhould be *more ſevere* than the other, ſome allowance will naturally be made for this ſuperior hardſhip; and the produce of one hour's

labour

labour in the one way may frequently exchange for that of two hours labour in the other.

Or if the one ſpecies of labour requires *an uncommon degree* of *dexterity* and *ingenuity*, the eſteem which men have for ſuch talents, will naturally give a value to their produce, ſuperior to what would be due to the time employed about it.—Such talents can ſeldom be acquired but in conſequence of long application, and the ſuperior value of their produce may frequently be no more than a reaſonable compenſation for the time and labour which muſt be ſpent in acquiring them.

In the price of CORN, *one part* pays the rent of the landlord, *another* pays the wages or maintenance of the labourers and labouring cattle employed in producing it, and *the third* pays the profit of the farmer.—Theſe *three* parts ſeem either immediately or ultimately to make up the *whole price* of corn.—A *fourth* part, it may perhaps be thought, is neceſſary for replacing the ſtock of the farmer, or for compenſating the wear and tear of his labouring cattle, and other inſtruments of huſbandry.

In the price of FLOUR or MEAL we muſt add to the price of the corn, the profits of the miller, and the wages of his ſervants; in the price of BREAD, the profits of the baker, and the wages of his ſervants; and in the price of *both*, the labour of transporting the corn from the house of the farmer to that of the miller, and from that of the miller to that of the baker, together with the profits of those who advance the wages of that labour.

The price of FLAX resolves itself into the same three parts as that of corn.—In the price of LINEN we must add to this price the wages of the flax-dresser, of the spinner, of the weaver, of the bleacher, &c. together with the profits of their respective employers.

A gentleman who *farms* a part of his own estate, after paying the expence of cultivation, should gain both the rent of the *landlord* and the profit of the *farmer*.—He is apt to denominate, however, his whole gain, *profit*, and thus confounds rent with profit, at least in common language.

Common farmers seldom employ any overseer to direct the general operations of the farm. They generally too work a good deal with their own hands, as ploughmen, harrowers, &c.—What remains of the crop after paying the rent, therefore, should not only replace to them their stock employed in cultivation, together with its ordinary profits, but pay them the wages which are due to them, both as *labourers* and *overseers*.—Whatever re-

mains,

mains, however, after paying the rent and keeping up the ſtock, is called profit,—but *wages* evidently make a part of it.—The farmer, *by ſaving theſe wages*, muſt neceſſarily *gain them*.—Wages, therefore, are in this caſe confounded with profit.

An *independent manufacturer*, who has ſtock enough both to purchaſe materials, and to maintain himſelf till he can carry his work to market, ſhould gain both the wages of a journeyman who works under a maſter, and the profit which that maſter makes by the ſale of the journeyman's work.—His whole gains, however, are commonly called profit, and wages are, in this caſe too, confounded with profit.

A *gardener* who cultivates his own garden with his own hands, unites in his own perſon the three different characters, of *landlord*, *farmer*, and *labourer*.—His produce, therefore, ſhould pay him the rent of the *firſt*, the profit of the *ſecond*, and the wages of the *third*.—The whole, however, is commonly conſidered as the earnings of his labour.—Both rent and profit are, in this caſe, confounded with wages.

An apothecary charges in his drugs he expence of his education, his houſe, his carriage if he has one, his conſtant attendance to the wiſhes of his employers, &c.—

But the whole is confounded in the idea of the value of the articles employed.

It is ſhameful to ſee the confuſion at preſent exiſting with reſpect to MEDICINE.—*Quacks* are riding in their coaches, while many of the *regular faculty* abſolutely ſtarve.—*Phyſicians* inſtead of directing the *apothecary* write now for the *druggiſt*, and *druggiſts* in return have uſurped the privilege of *medical advice.*—*Man-midwives* and *dentiſts* call themſelves *ſurgeons.*—*Apothecaries*, nay *ſurgeons*, preſcribe like *phyſicians*, and accept the fee as ſuch, and we find, *even* in capital towns, the union of OCCULIST—SURGEON—DENTIST—MAN-MIDWIFE—APOTHECARY—and DRUGGIST, in the ſame perſon, which deſtroys altogether the advantage which reſults to ſociety from the *proper diſtribution of labour.*

Why does not government interfere in regulating the practice of medicine?—The *chemiſt*, by not including *medical advice*, ſhould demand leſs than the *apothecary*, who includes his attendance and ſkill in the drug. It would be certainly much to the advantage of the public, were the employments of *druggiſt* and *apothecary* ſeparate, were the latter INSPECTORS of the ſhops of the former, and only, in fact, MEDICAL ADVISERS.—Drugs would not then be improperly heaped on the patient,

and

and the *apothecary* and *physician* might ſtill be diſtinguiſhed, by their education and fee.—The fears of colluſion between the *doctor* and *apothecary*, too often unjuſtly entertained, would ceaſe, and *the practice of medicine would be put on a more liberal and gentleman-like footing* *.

* Adam Smith.

SECT. XI.

OF THE PRINCIPLE OF TRADE.

THIS division of labour, from which so many advantages are derived, is not originally the effect of any human wisdom, which foresees and intends that general opulence to which it gives occasion.—It is the necessary, though very slow and gradual, consequence of a certain propensity in human nature which has in view no such extensive utility; it arises from *self-love.*

In civilized society man stands at all times in need of the co-operation and assistance of great multitudes, while his *whole life* is scarce sufficient to gain the *friendship* of a few persons.—In almost every other race of animals, each individual, when it is grown up to maturity, is entirely independent, and in its natural state has occasion for the assistance of no other living creature.—*But man has almost constant occasion for the help of his brethren*, and it is in vain for him to expect it from *their benevolence*

only.

only.—He will be more likely to prevail if he can intereſt their SELF-LOVE in his favour, and ſhew them that it is for *their own advantage* to do for him what he requires of them.—Whoever offers to another a bargain of any kind, propoſes to do this: "*Give me that which I want, and you ſhall have this which you want*," is the meaning of every ſuch offer; and it is in this manner that we obtain from one another the far greater part of thoſe good offices which we ſtand in need of.—It is not from the *benevolence* of the *butcher*, the *brewer*, or the *baker*, that we *expect* our *dinner*, but from their regard to their own intereſt.—We addreſs ourſelves, not to their *humanity*, but to their *ſelf-love*; and never talk to them of *our own neceſſities*, but of their *advantages*.—Nobody but a beggar chooſes to depend chiefly upon the benevolence of his fellow-citizens.—Even a beggar does not depend upon it entirely.—The charity of well-diſpoſed people, indeed, ſupplies him with the whole fund of his ſubſiſtence.—But though this principle ultimately provides him with them as he has occaſion for them, the greater part of *his* occaſional wants are *ſupplied in the ſame manner* as thoſe of other people, by *treaty*, by *barter*, and by *purchaſe*.—With the money which one man gives him he purchaſes food.—The old clothes which another bestows upon him he exchanges for other old clothes which suit him better, or for lodging, or for food, or for money, with which he can buy either food, clothes, or lodging, as he has occasion *.

* Adam Smith.

In the same manner our government (as was shewn in the chapter on the Reform of Parliament) depends not on the *patriotism* of the legislature: but on a more *certain foundation*—SELF-INTEREST—or *the balance of powers.* This is not said to *decry* virtue: *for honesty is the best policy, and when we deviate from the path of rectitude we act against our proper interest.* There is undoubtedly a certain kind of *honour* in trade, or fear of universal censure, and of the resentment of the injured: but for all this, it is argued, that the *general* principle of trade is not generosity and humanity, or Christian philanthropy, but SELF-INTEREST; nor can it be imputed as a crime, that a man loves himself better than a neighbour, or perhaps a stranger, who has obliged him in nothing. To make every thing *run even*, the spring of activity should be such as has an influence on all descriptions of men.

SECT.

SECT. XII.

ON LUXURY.

LUXURY is a word of an uncertain signification, and may be taken in a *good* as well as in a *bad sense*.—In general, it means great refinement in the gratification of the senses; and *any degree of it* may be *innocent* or *blameable*, according to the age, or country, or condition of the person.—The bounds between virtue and vice cannot here be exactly fixed.—To imagine, that the gratifying of any sense, or the indulging of any delicacy in meat, drink, or apparel, is of itself a vice, can never enter into a head that is not disordered by the frenzies of enthusiasm.—I have, indeed, heard of a monk abroad, who, because the windows of his cell opened upon a noble prospect, made a covenant with his eyes never to turn that way, or receive *so sensual a gratification*.—And such is the crime of drinking Champagne or Burgundy, preferable to small beer or porter.—*These indulgences are only vices, when they are pursued at the expence of some virtue,*

tue, as liberality or charity; in like manner as they are follies, when for them a man ruins his fortune, and reduces himself to want and beggary.—Where they entrench upon no virtue, but leave ample subject whence to provide for friends, family, and every proper object of generosity or compassion, they are entirely innocent, and have in every age been acknowledged such by almost all moralists.

Human happiness, according to the most received notions, seems to consist in three ingredients;

Action,

Pleasure, and

Indolence.

And though these ingredients ought to be mixed in different proportions, according to the particular disposition of the person; yet no one ingredient can be entirely wanting, without destroying, in some measure, the relish of the whole composition.—*Indolence*, or repose, indeed, seems not of itself to contribute much to our enjoyment; but, like sleep, is requisite as an indulgence to the weakness of human nature, which cannot support an uninterrupted course of business or pleasure.—That quick march of the spirits, which takes a man from himself, and chiefly gives satisfaction, does in the end exhaust the mind, and requires some intervals of

repose,

repose, which, though agreeable for a moment, yet, if prolonged, beget a languor and lethargy, that destroys all enjoyment.—Education, custom, and example, have a mighty influence in turning the mind to any of these pursuits; and it must be owned, that, where they promote a relish for *action* and *pleasure*, they are so far favourable to human happiness.—*In times when industry and the arts flourish, men are kept in perpetual occupation, and enjoy, as their reward,* THE OCCUPATION ITSELF, *as well as* THOSE PLEASURES *which are the fruit of their labour.*—The mind acquires new vigour; enlarges its powers and faculties; and by an assiduity in honest industry, both satisfies its natural appetites, and prevents the growth of unnatural ones, which commonly spring up, when nourished by ease and idleness.—Banish those arts from society, you deprive men both of action and of pleasure; and leaving nothing but indolence in their place, you even destroy the relish of indolence, which never is agreeable, but when it succeeds to labour, and recruits the spirits, exhausted by too much application and fatigue.

Another advantage of industry and of refinements in the mechanical arts, is, that they commonly produce some refinements in the *liberal*; nor can one be carried to perfection, without being accompanied, in ſome degree, with the other.—The ſame age, which abounds with ſkilful weavers and ſhip-carpenters, uſually produces great philoſophers and politicians, renowned generals and poets.—The ſpi.it of the age affects all the arts; and the minds of men, being once rouſed from their lethargy, and put into a fermentation, turn themſelves on all ſides, and carry improvements into every art and ſcience.—*Profound ignorance* is totally baniſhed, and men enjoy the privilege of rational creatures, to think as well as to act, to cultivate the pleaſures of the mind as well as thoſe of the body.

The more theſe refined arts advance, the more *ſociable* men become; nor is it poſſible, that, when enriched with ſcience, and poſſeſſed of a fund of converſation, they ſhould be contented to remain in ſolitude, or live with their fellow-citizens in that diſtant manner, which is peculiar to ignorant and barbarous nations.—They flock into cities; love to receive and communicate knowledge; to ſhew their wit or their breeding; their taſte in converſation or living, in clothes or furniture.—Curioſity allures the wiſe; vanity the fooliſh; and pleaſure both.—Particular clubs and ſocieties are every where formed: both ſexes meet in an eaſy and ſociable man-

ner;

ner; and the tempers of men, as well as their behaviour, refine apace.—So that, beside the improvements which they receive from knowledge and the liberal arts, it is impossible but they must feel an increase of humanity, from the very habit of conversing together, and contributing to each other's pleasure and entertainment. Thus INDUSTRY, KNOWLEDGE, and HUMANITY, are linked together by an *indissoluble* chain, and are found, from experience as well as reason, to be *peculiar* to the *more polished*, and, what are commonly denominated, *the more luxurious ages.*

Nor are THESE ADVANTAGES attended with *disadvantages*, that bear *any proportion to them.*—The more men refine upon pleasure, the less will they indulge in excesses of any kind; because nothing is more destructive to true pleasure than such excesses.—One may safely affirm, that the *Tartars* are oftener guilty of *beastly gluttony*, when they feast on their dead horses, than *European courtiers* with all their refinements of cookery.—And if libertine love, or even infidelity to the marriage-bed, be more frequent in polite ages; *drunkenness*, on the other hand, is much less common.

But INDUSTRY, KNOWLEDGE, and HUMANITY, are not advantageous in *private life* alone: they diffuse their beneficial influence on *the public*, and render the government as great and flouriſhing as they make individuals happy and proſperous.—The increaſe and conſumption of all the commodities, which ſerve to the ornament and pleaſure of life, are advantageous to ſociety; becauſe, at the ſame time that they multiply thoſe innocent gratifications to individuals, they are a kind of ſtorehouſe of labour, which, in the exigencies of ſtate, may be turned to the public ſervice.—In a nation, where there is no demand for ſuch ſuperfluities, men ſink into indolence, loſe all enjoyment of life, and are uſeleſs to the public, which cannot maintain or ſupport its fleets and armies, from the induſtry of ſuch ſlothful members.

The bounds of all the *European* kingdoms are, at preſent, nearly the ſame they were two hundred years ago: *but what a difference is there in the power and grandeur of thoſe kingdoms?* Which can be aſcribed to nothing but the increaſe of art and induſtry.—When CHARLES VIII. of France invaded Italy, he carried with him about 20,000 men: yet this armament ſo exhauſted the nation, as we learn from Guicciardin, that for ſome years it was not able to make any great effort.—LOUIS XIV. in time of war, kept in pay above 400,000 men †;

† The inſcription on the Place-de Vendome ſays 440,000.

though

though from Mazarine's death to his own, he was engaged in a courfe of wars that lafted near thirty years.

This induftry is much promoted by the knowledge infeparable from ages of art and refinement; as, on the other hand, this knowledge enables the public to make the beft advantage of the induftry of its fubjects.—Laws, order, police, difcipline; thefe can never be carried to any degree of perfection, before human reafon has refined itfelf by exercife, and by an application to the more vulgar arts, at leaft, of *commerce* and *manufacture*.—Can we expect, that a government will be well modelled by a people, who know not how to make a fpinning-wheel, or to employ a loom to advantage? Not to mention, that all ignorant ages are infefted with fuperftition, which throws the government off its bias, and difturbs men in the purfuit of their intereft and happinefs.

Knowledge in the arts of government naturally begets mildnefs and moderation, by inftructing men in the advantages of *humane maxims* above rigour and feverity, which drive fubjects into rebellion, and make the return to fubmiffion impracticable, by cutting off all hopes of pardon.—When the tempers of men are foftened as well

as

as their knowledge improved, *this humanity* appears ſtill more conſpicuous, and is the chief characteriſtic which diſtinguiſhes a civilized age from times of barbarity and ignorance.—*Factions are then leſs inveterate, revolutions leſs tragical, authority leſs ſevere, and ſeditions leſs frequent.—Even foreign wars abate of their cruelty; and after the field of battle, where honour and intereſt ſteel men againſt compaſſion as well as fear, the combatants diveſt themſelves of the brute, and reſume the man.*

Nor need we fear, that men, by loſing their ferocity, will loſe their martial ſpirit, or become leſs undaunted and vigorous in defence of their country or their liberty.—The arts have no ſuch effect in enervating either the mind or body.—On the contrary, induſtry, their inſeparable attendant, adds new force to both.—And if anger, which is ſaid to be the whetſtone of courage, loſes ſomewhat of its aſperity, by politeneſs and refinement; *a ſenſe of honour*, which is a ſtronger, more conſtant, and more governable principle, acquires freſh vigour by that elevation of genius which ariſes from knowledge and a good education.—Add to this, that courage can neither have any duration, nor be of any uſe, when not accompanied with diſcipline and martial ſkill, which are ſeldom found among a barbarous people.—The ancients remarked, that *Datames* was the only barbarian that ever knew the art of war.—And *Pyrrhus*, ſeeing the ROMANS marſhal their army with ſome art and ſkill, ſaid with ſurpriſe, "*Theſe barbarians have nothing barbarous in their diſcipline!*"

What has chiefly induced ſevere moraliſts to declaim againſt refinement in the arts, is the example of *ancient Rome*, which, joining to its poverty and ruſticity, virtue and public ſpirit, roſe to ſuch a ſurpriſing height of grandeur and liberty; but having learned from its conquered provinces *the Aſiatic luxury*, fell into every kind of corruption; whence aroſe *ſedition* and *civil wars*, attended at laſt with *the total loſs of liberty*.—All the Latin claſſics, whom we peruſe in our infancy, are full of theſe ſentiments, and univerſally aſcribe the ruin of their ſtate to the arts and riches imported from the eaſt: inſomuch that SALLUST repreſents a taſte for *painting* as a vice, no leſs than *lewdneſs* and *drinking*.—And ſo popular were theſe ſentiments, during the later ages of the republic, that this author abounds in praiſes of the old *rigid Roman virtue*, though himſelf the moſt egregious inſtance of modern luxury and corruption: ſpeaks contemptuouſly of the Grecian eloquence, though the moſt elegant writer in the world; nay, employs prepoſterous digreſ-

ſions

ſions and declamations to this purpoſe, though a model of taſte and correctneſs.

But it would be eaſy to prove, that theſe writers *miſtook* the cauſe of the diſorders in the Roman ſtate, and *aſcribed* to *luxury* and *the arts*, what really proceeded from an *ill-modelled government*, and *the unlimited extent of conqueſts*.—Refinement on the pleaſures and conveniencies of life has no natural tendency to beget venality and corruption.—The value, which all men put upon any particular pleaſure, depends on compariſon and experience; nor is a porter leſs greedy of money, which he ſpends on bacon and brandy, than a courtier who purchaſes champagne and ortolans.—*Riches are valuable at all times, and to all men; becauſe they always purchaſe pleaſures, ſuch as men are accuſtomed to, and deſire: nor can any thing reſtrain or regulate the love of money, but a ſenſe of honour and honeſty; which, if it be not nearly equal at all times, will naturally abound moſt in ages of knowledge and refinement.*

The liberties of ENGLAND, ſo far from decaying ſince the improvements in the arts, have never flouriſhed ſo much as during that period.—*And though corruption may ſeem to increaſe of late years; this is chiefly to be aſcribed to our eſtabliſhed liberty, when our princes have found the im-*

poſſibility

possibility of governing without parliaments, or of terrifying parliaments by the phantom of prerogative.—Not to mention, that this corruption or venality prevails much more among the *electors* than the elected; and therefore cannot justly be ascribed to any refinements in luxury.

If we consider the matter in a proper light, we shall find, that a progress in the arts is rather favourable to *liberty*, and has a natural tendency to *preserve*, if not produce, a FREE GOVERNMENT.—In rude unpolished nations, where the arts are neglected, all labour is bestowed on the cultivation of the ground; and the whole society is divided into two classes, *proprietors of land*, and their *vassals* or *tenants*.—The *latter* are necessarily dependent, and fitted for slavery and subjection; especially where they possess no riches, and are not valued for their knowledge in agriculture; as must always be the case where the arts are neglected.—The *former* naturally erect themselves into petty tyrants; and must either submit to an absolute master, for the sake of peace and order; or, if they will preserve their independency, like the ancient barons, they must fall into feuds and contests among themselves, and throw the whole society into such confusion, as is perhaps worse than the most despotic government.—*But where luxury nourishes commerce and industry, the peasants, by a proper cultivation of the land, become rich and independent; while the tradesmen and merchants acquire a share of the property, and draw authority and consideration to that middling rank of men, who are the best and firmest basis of public liberty.*—These submit not to slavery, like the peasants, from poverty and meanness of spirit; and, having no hopes of tyrannizing over others, like the barons, they are not tempted, for the sake of that gratification, to submit to the tyranny of their sovereign.—They covet *equal laws*, which may secure their property, and preserve them from *monarchical*, as well as *aristocratical tyranny**.

UPON THE WHOLE IT APPEARS THEN, THE LABOURS OF AN INDUSTRIOUS AND INGENIOUS PEOPLE IN CIVILIZED COUNTRIES ARE VARIOUSLY, BUT INCESSANTLY EMPLOYED, IN THE SERVICE OF THE RICH.—IN THEIR DRESS, THEIR TABLE, THEIR HOUSES, AND THEIR FURNITURE, THE FAVOURITES OF FORTUNE UNITE EVERY REFINEMENT OF CONVENIENCY, OF ELEGANCE, AND OF SPLENDOUR; WHATEVER CAN SOOTH THEIR PRIDE, OR GRATIFY THEIR SENSUALITY.—SUCH REFINEMENTS UNDER THE ODI-

* HUME.

OUS NAME OF LUXURY, HAVE BEEN SEVERELY ARRAIGNED BY THE MORALISTS OF EVERY AGE; BUT IN THE PRESENT IMPERFECT CONDITION OF SOCIETY, LUXURY, THOUGH IT MAY PROCEED FROM VICE OR FOLLY AND OCCASION THEM, SEEMS TO BE THE ONLY LIKELY MEANS TO PROMOTE THE INDUSTRY OF OTHERS, AND CORRECT THE UNEQUAL* DISTRIBUTION OF PROPERTY.—THE DILIGENT MECHANIC, AND THE SKILFUL ARTIST, WHO HAVE OBTAINED NO SHARE IN THE DIVISION OF THE EARTH, RECEIVE A VOLUNTARY TAX FROM THE POSSESSORS OF GREAT ESTATES; AND THE LATTER ARE PROMPTED, BY A SENSE OF INTEREST, TO IMPROVE THOSE LANDS, WITH WHOSE PRODUCE THEY MAY BE ENABLED TO PURCHASE ADDITIONAL PLEASURES.

SECT.

* It muſt, indeed, be confeſſed, that nature is ſo liberal to mankind, *that were all her preſents equally divided among the ſpecies, and improved by art and induſtry, every individual would enjoy all the neceſſaries, and even moſt of the comforts of life; nor would ever be liable to any ills, but ſuch as might accidentally ariſe from the ſickly frame and conſtitution of his body.*—It muſt be confeſſed, wherever we depart from the EQUALITY, we rob the *poor* of *more ſatisfaction* than we *add* to the *rich*, and that the *ſlight gratification* of a *frivolous vanity*, in ONE individual, frequently coſts more than *bread* to MANY FAMILIES, and EVEN PROVINCES.

But hiſtorians, alas! and even common ſenſe, may inform us, however

 ſpecious

SECT. XIII.

ON LIBERTY AS CONNECTED WITH TRADE.

THE *arts* and *manufactures*, *trade* and *commerce*, are inſeparably connected with FREEDOM; *they ariſe* from IT; and *they* tend to *produce* IT.—Let any country *regain* its LIBERTY, and *theſe return*; let a country *loſe* its LIBERTY, and *theſe* gradually *die away*; let *them flouriſh*, and the country cannot eaſily be *ſubdued* by a *foreign power*, nor *enſlaved* by *its own ſovereign*.—*Artiſts*, *manufacturers*, and *merchants*, are the *life* and *ſoul* of LIBER-

ſpecious theſe *levelling ideas*, they are really, at bottom, *impracticable*; and were they not ſo, would be extremely *pernicious* to human ſociety.

Render poſſeſſions ever ſo *equal*, men's different degrees of art, care, and induſtry, will immediately break *that equality*.—Or if you *check theſe virtues*, you reduce ſociety to the extremeſt indigence; and inſtead of preventing *want* and *beggary* in a *few*, render it *unavoidable* to the *whole community*.—The moſt rigorous inquiſition, too, is requiſite to watch every inequality on its firſt appearance; and the moſt ſevere juriſdiction, to puniſh and redreſs it.—But beſides, that *ſo much authority* muſt ſoon degenerate into *tyranny*, and be exerted with *great partialities*; and who can poſſibly be poſſeſſed of it in the *ſavage ſtate* here ſuppoſed? HUME.——(This by the bye, that the meaning of the laſt paragraph may not be miſunderſtood.)

TY; the metropolis is the chief vital part, where the firſt and the laſt pulſe of LIBERTY will be felt.

Under a deſpotic government, property is precarious, wealth is dangerous; it is not the intereſt of the deſpot to encourage trade, nor is it the intereſt of merchants and manufacturers to truſt a deſpot.

The moſt fertile country, if the government is not free, will not allure them; ſecurity of property, and certainty of enjoyment, being their firſt reſearch, theſe bees often lodge their honey in the barren rock.—The *Tyrians* by commerce acquired ſuch wealth and ſtrength, as enabled them for thirteen years to reſiſt the whole power of NEBUCHADNEZZAR; rather than ſubmit at laſt, they quitted a fertile country, and retired to a little iſland, where they built their city on a rock, and there maintained their freedom.—*Marſeilles* is ſurrounded by a barren country.—The cities of *Holland* are encloſed by marſhes, and *Venice* by the ſea.

At the commencement of the eleventh century, EUROPE began to *awake* as out of a deep ſleep; the eyes of its inhabitants were opened to ſee the *utility* of COMMERCE, with the *value* of LIBERTY, and their *mutual connection*.—They had borne the yoke of *feodal* tyranny for many ages.—That ſyſtem of government was very

very ſimple, but to the laſt degree oppreſſive.—The ſovereign ſometimes exerted deſpotic ſway over the feodal lords; at other times, indeed, his power was circumſcribed, and his authority deſpiſed; but the feodal lords themſelves exerciſed at *all times* the moſt abſolute dominion over their ſlaves and vaſſals.—Cities being ſubject to the juriſdiction and oppreſſion of the lords, and deſerted by merchants and manufacturers, were inhabited only by ſlaves, and the loweſt of the people.—The active and induſtrious artiſts were driven away by the impolitic exactions, and abſurd regulations of the avaricious barons.—In the eleventh century, ſome cities in *Italy* caſt off the yoke, others purchaſed their freedom, and eſtabliſhed an equal government.—The cities of *France*, *Germany*, *Spain*, and *England*, ſoon followed the example.

In the *train* of *returning* LIBERTY, came the *arts*, *manufactures*, *commerce*, *induſtry*, and *wealth*.—Happy had it been for mankind, if luxury could have been left behind.—Even luxury, under the reſtraint of reaſon and religion, is beneficial to ſociety, promotes induſtry, and leads to the perfection of the arts.

At the introduction of commerce, the cities of *Italy* took the lead, and ſoon eſtabliſhed their freedom and independence;

dependence; among these was *Florence*, by whose government, under the form of a democracy, encouraging and protecting manufactures, this city grew in power, and its citizens in wealth.

Venice is more ancient and honourable than *Florence*. *Venice* is governed by a peculiar kind of aristocracy, whose interest is to encourage commerce, because her nobility engage in it.—*Jealous of her liberty, she employs only foreign mercenaries in her army, while her navy, which is her chief strength, is manned and commanded by her own subjects.*—By her traffic she acquired such wealth and power, as enabled her, in the beginning of the sixteenth century, to resist the united efforts of the *Pope*, the *Emperor* of *Germany*, the *kings* of *France* and *Arragon*, with almost *all the princes of Italy*.—It matters not what free form of government is adopted by any country, democracy, or mixed monarchy, provided the artists, manufacturers, and merchants, can find a spot where they may enjoy peace and quietness, protection and security for their persons and possessions.—We have had examples of the two first; let us consider an instance of the latter.—The *Seventeen Provinces* of the *Netherlands* were first united under *Philip of Burgundy*, in the beginning of the fifteenth century.—They had long en-

 joyed

joyed the ſweets of a free government, ſimilar to that eſtabliſhed in all the northern nations.—The ſovereignty was hereditary, but the laws were paſſed, and taxes voted, by the three eſtates of the nobility, the clergy, and the commons.—Their cities had peculiar immunities and internal juriſdiction.—This ſecurity and happineſs was not diſturbed by *Philip*.—This prince being *wiſe*, conſidered, that the wealth which flowed into his dominions through the cities of *Bourges*, *Ghent*, and *Antwerp*, would ceaſe to flow, ſhould theſe cities loſe their LIBERTY; being *good*, HE LOVED HIS SUBJECTS, AND REJOICED TO SEE THEM HAPPY.—When therefore by their blood and treaſure he had eſtabliſhed his throne, and ſecured himſelf againſt the power of *France*, HE WAS CONTENTED TO REIGN OVER A FREE PEOPLE; KNOWING THAT THE HAPPINESS OF THE SUBJECT IS THE SUREST FOUNDATION OF THE SOVEREIGN'S GREATNESS.

The emperor *Charles* the Vth, being a native of the *Low Countries*, had a peculiar love for this part of his dominions; which, during his reign, continued to increaſe in wealth.—*Philip* the IId, his ſucceſſor in the *Netherlands* and *Spain*, being a prince of different diſpoſitions, and reſiding in *Spain*, his native country, appointed *the Duchess* of *Parma* regent of the *Low Countries*, with orders to set up THE INQUISITION *.—The common

* The *prisons* of the inquisition are little dark cells, without any furniture but a hard quilt: the *prisoner* is not permitted to see any one except his keeper, in this cell, who brings his diet with a lamp that burns half an hour, and departs in silence. At the end of three days he is carried to the *inquisitor*, and takes an oath to return true answers to all questions which shall be put to him, and to confess all his heresies. If he have no heresies to confess, he is carried back to his doleful dungeon for three days more, to recollect himself, and to call to mind his heresies, his teachers, and his accomplices. Being again brought before the inquisitors, they ask him where he was born and educated; who were his parents, masters, confessor; when he was last at confession, or the mass? If, in answering all these questions, he cannot be brought to accuse himself, he is sent back again to his dark and dismal prison, and time is given him to pray for repentance. At the end of three days he is carried again to the inquisitors, who now examine him on the peculiar doctrines of popery, on transubstantiation, on worshipping the host, images, saints, and the Virgin Mary; on the infallibility of the pope, and his power to pardon sins past, present, and to come, &c. &c. If he answers, *that he believes all this*, he is then taken to the rack, attended by a *notary*, who is to write down his confession. Here he remains in torment for one hour by the glass, after which a *surgeon* puts his bones in joint, and he is carried back to his cell. And this horrid process is repeated three times, at certain intervals, till the miserable wretch perhaps confesses heresies he was never guilty of, or acknowledges that he dare not worship idols. If, after two days, the prisoner affirms that his confession was extorted from him by the torments he underwent, and therefore refuses to sign it; he is again put upon the rack. If he confesses that he did speak heretical words, but to save his estate for his family, affirms that he spake them unadvisedly; he is put upon the rack to prove the truth of this assertion. The prisoner never knows who are his accusers, or what particular words or actions are laid to his charge; nor must his advocate know these things. Witnesses are compelled to give evidence, under pain of the greater excommunication; and his own advocate is bound by oath to divulge his

common people revolted, but were soon reduced.—To punish them, to insure the establishment of the inquisition, and to prevent any future insurrections, *Philip* sent a reinforcement to the Duchess, consisting of ten thousand veteran soldiers, Spanish and Italian, under the command of the *Duke* of *Alva*, an experienced general. —This force produced astonishment, submission, and despair, among those who could not fly before it.—"*Upon the first report of this expedition, the trading people of the towns and country began in vast numbers to retire out of the provinces; so as the duchess wrote to the king, that in a few days above a hundred thousand men had left the coun-*

client's secrets. When the fatal morning is come, the dominicans begin the procession, followed by the penitents clothed in black, barefooted, and with wax candles in their hands; some have benitoes, and others who have but just escaped being burnt, have inverted flames painted on their garments: then come the negative and relapsed, with flames pointed upwards; then the professed, with flames painted on their garments and on their breasts, carrying their own pictures, with dogs, serpents, and devils round them, all with open mouths. The *familiars* and *inquisitors* close the procession. After prayers and a sermon, the prisoners are delivered over to the secular arm, with earnest entreaties not to touch their blood, or put their life in danger! They are instantly bound with chains, carried to the secular prison for about two hours, then brought out, chained to stakes about four yards high, seated within half a yard of the top, when the negative and relapsed are strangled, but the honest and professed are solemnly delivered up to the devil; after which the holy fathers leave them: when, their faces being first scorched, the furze is kindled round them, and in about half an hour in calm weather, or in about two hours in very windy weather, their excruciating torments end. Dr. Geddes.

try,

try, and withdrawn both their money and their goods, and more were following every day: so great an antipathy there ever appears between merchants and soldiers."—Many of these families came to *England*, and settled in *Norwich*, *Colchester*, *Sandwich*, *Maidstone*, and *Southampton*, under protection of Queen *Elizabeth*.—In return for their hospitable reception, they enriched the kingdom with the manufacture of bays, and other linen and woollen cloths of like kind *.—Some of them settled in *Sweden*, and carried the iron and other manufactures into that country †.—*Fresh exactions, cruelties, and oppressions, excited in the* NETHERLANDS *fresh insurrections, which never more subsided till after a contest, which lasted upwards of forty years, the* SEVEN UNITED PROVINCES *established their liberty, and were acknowledged a free and independent people.—The arts, manufactures, and commerce, returned with returning liberty, and wealth flowed in upon them from every quarter of the globe.*

If for a moment we can turn away our eyes from this scene of industry, from these rich provinces, where peace and plenty reign, let us enquire what is become of *Athens*, *Tyre*, *Sidon*, *Carthage*, *Colchis*, *Syracuse*,

* Camden, p. 416.

† Lord Molesworth's Account of Denmark and Sweden.

Agrigentum, *Rhodes*, those free cities, each of which in its day has been the metropolis of the commercial world? They are now no more, their place is hardly to be found.—*They lost their liberty*, and *with liberty* the *arts*, *manufactures*, and *commerce*, have taken their *everlasting flight* *.

* TOWNSEND.

SECT.

SECT. XIV.

ON AGRICULTURE.

THE *final view* of all RATIONAL POLITICS is to produce *the greateſt quantity of happineſs* in a given tract of country.—The riches, ſtrength, and glory of nations, the topics which hiſtory celebrates, and which alone almoſt engage the praiſes, and poſſeſs the admiration of mankind, have no value farther than as they contribute to *this end*.—When they interfere with it, they are evils, and not the leſs real for the ſplendour that ſurrounds them.

Secondly, although we ſpeak of communities as of ſentient beings; although we aſcribe to them happineſs and miſery, deſires, intereſts, and paſſions, nothing really exiſts or feels but *individuals*.—*The happineſs of a people* is made up of the happineſs of *ſingle perſons*; and the quantity of happineſs can only be augmented by increaſing the happineſs of individuals.

The fertility of the ground, in temperate regions, is

capable of being improved by *cultivation* to an extent which is unknown: much, however, beyond the ſtate of improvement in any country in EUROPE.—In our own, which holds almoſt the firſt place in the knowledge and encouragement of *agriculture*, let it only be ſuppoſed that every field in ENGLAND of the ſame original quality with thoſe in the neighbourhood of the metropolis, and conſequently capable of the ſame fertility, were by a like management made to yield an equal produce, and it may be aſſerted, I believe, with truth, that the quantity of human proviſion raiſed in the iſland would be increaſed *fivefold*.—The two principles, therefore, upon which population ſeems primarily to depend, *the fecundity of the ſpecies*, and *the capacity of the ſoil*, would in moſt, perhaps in all countries, enable it to proceed much further than it has yet advanced.—The number of marriageable women, who, in each country, remain unmarried, afford a computation how much the agency of nature in the diffuſion of human life is cramped and contracted; and *the quantity of waſte*, *neglected*, or *miſmanaged ſurface*, together with a comparison, like the preceding, of the crops raiſed from the ſoil in the neighbourhood of populous cities, and under a perfect ſtate of cultivation, with thoſe, which lands

of

of equal or ſuperior quality yield in different ſituations, will ſhew in what proportion the indigenous productions of the earth *are capable of being further augmented.*

In CHINA, where the inhabitants frequent the ſea ſhore, and ſubſiſt in a great meaſure upon *fiſh*, the population is deſcribed to be exceſſive.—This peculiarity ariſes, not probably from any civil advantages, any care or policy, any particular conſtitution or ſuperior wiſdom of government, but ſimply from hence, that the ſpecies of food, to which cuſtom hath reconciled the deſires and inclinations of the inhabitants, is that which, of all others, is procured in the greateſt abundance, with the moſt eaſe, and ſtands in need of the leaſt preparation.

The natives of INDOSTAN, being confined, by the laws of their religion, to the uſe of *vegetable food*, and requiring little except rice, which the country produces in plentiful crops; and food, in warm climates, compoſing the only want of life; theſe countries are populous, under all the injuries of a deſpotic, and the agitations of an unſettled government.—If any revolution, or what would be called perhaps refinement of manners, ſhould generate in theſe people *a taſte for the fleſh of animals*, ſimilar to what prevails amongſt the Arabian

hordes;

hordes; ſhould introduce flocks and herds into grounds which are now covered with corn; ſhould teach them to account a certain portion of this ſpecies of food amongſt the neceſſaries of life; the population, from this ſingle change, would ſuffer in a few years a great diminution: and this diminution would follow, in ſpite of every effort of the laws, or even of any improvement that might take place in their civil condition.

The firſt reſource of *ſavage life* is in the fleſh of WILD ANIMALS; hence the numbers amongſt ſavage nations, compared with the tract of country which they occupy, are univerſally ſmall, becauſe this ſpecies of proviſion is, of all others, ſupplied in the ſlendereſt proportion.—*The next ſtep* was the invention of PASTURAGE, or the rearing of flocks and herds of tame animals.—*This alteration* added to the ſtock of proviſion much: but *the laſt* and *principal improvement* was to follow, namely, TILLAGE, or the artificial production of corn, eſculent plants, and roots.

So far as the ſtate of population is governed and limited by the quantity of proviſion, perhaps there is no ſingle cauſe that affects it ſo powerfully, as the kind and quality of food, which chance or uſage hath introduced into a country.—In ENGLAND, notwithſtanding the produce

produce of the ſoil has been, of late, conſiderably *increaſed*, by the incloſure of waſtes, and the adoption, in many places, of a more ſucceſsful huſbandry, yet we do not obſerve a correſponding addition to the number of inhabitants; the reaſon of which appears to me to be the more general conſumption of *animal food* amongſt us.—Many ranks of people, whoſe ordinary diet was, in the laſt century, prepared almoſt entirely from milk, roots, and vegetables, now require every day a conſiderable portion of the fleſh of animals.—Hence a great part of the richeſt lands of the country are converted to paſturage.—Much alſo of the bread corn, which went directly to the nouriſhment of human bodies, now only contributes to it, by fattening the fleſh of ſheep and oxen.—The maſs and volume of proviſions are hereby *diminiſhed*; and what is gained in the melioration of the ſoil is loſt in the quality of the produce.—This conſideration teaches us, that TILLAGE, as an object of national care and encouragement, is univerſally preferable to *paſturage*; becauſe *the kind of proviſion* which it yields goes *much further* in the ſuſtention of human life.—TILLAGE is alſo recommended by this additional advantage, that it affords *employment* to a much more *numerous peaſantry*.—Indeed *paſturage* ſeems to be the art of a nation,

 either

either imperfectly civilized, as are many of the tribes which cultivate it in the internal parts of ASIA; or of a nation, like SPAIN, declining from its ſummit by luxury and inactivity.

The kind and quality of proviſion, together with the extent and capacity of the ſoil from which it is raiſed, being the ſame; the quantity procured will principally depend upon two circumſtances, the *ability* of the occupier, and *the encouragement* which he receives.—The greateſt misfortune of a country is an indigent tenantry.—Whatever be the native advantages of the ſoil, or even the ſkill and induſtry of the occupier, the want of *a ſufficient capital* confines every plan, as well as cripples and weakens every operation of huſbandry.—This evil is felt where agriculture is accounted a ſervile or mean employment: where farms are *extremely ſubdivided*, and badly furniſhed with habitations; where leaſes are unknown, or are of ſhort or precarious duration.—With reſpect to the *encouragement* of huſbandry; in this, as in every other employment, the true reward of induſtry is in the price and ſale of the produce.—The excluſive right to the produce is the only incitement which acts conſtantly and univerſally; the only ſpring which keeps human labour in motion.—ALL THEREFORE THAT THE LAWS

CAN DO, IS TO SECURE THIS RIGHT TO THE OCCUPIER OF THE GROUND, THAT IS, TO CONSTITUTE SUCH A SYSTEM OF TENURE, THAT THE FULL AND ENTIRE ADVANTAGE OF EVERY IMPROVEMENT GO TO THE BENEFIT OF THE IMPROVER; THAT EVERY MAN WORK FOR HIMSELF, AND NOT FOR ANOTHER; AND THAT NO MAN SHARE IN THE PROFIT WHO DOES NOT ASSIST IN THE PRODUCTION.

No man can purchase without an equivalent, and that equivalent, by the generality of the people, must, in every country, be derived from employment. And upon this basis is founded the public benefit of *trade*, that is to say, its subserviency to increase the quantity of food, in which its only real utility consists.—Of that industry, and of those arts and branches of trade, which are employed in the production, conveyance, and preparation of any principal species of human food, as of the business of the husbandman, the butcher, baker, brewer, corn-merchant, &c. we acknowledge the necessity: likewise of those manufactures which furnish us with warm clothing, convenient habitations, domestic utensils, as of the weaver, taylor, smith, carpenter, &c. we perceive (in climates, however, like ours, removed at a distance from the sun) the conduciveness to happinefs, by their rendering human life more healthy, vigorous, and comfortable.—*But not one half of the occupations which compofe the trade of Europe fall within either of thefe defcriptions.*—Perhaps two thirds of the manufacturers of England are employed upon articles of confeffed luxury, ornament, or fplendour: in the fuperfluous embellifhment of fome articles which are ufeful in their kind, or upon others which have no conceivable ufe or value, but what is founded in caprice or fafhion.—What can be lefs neceffary, or lefs connected with the fuftention of human life, than the whole produce of the filk, lace, and plate manufactory?—yet *what multitudes* labour in the different branches of thefe arts!—What can be imagined more capricious than the fondnefs for tobacco and fnuff?—yet how many various occupations, and *how many thoufands* in each, are fet at work in adminiftering to this frivolous gratification!—Concerning trades of this kind, and this kind comprehends more than half of the trades that are exercifed, it may fairly be afked, "*how, fince they add nothing to the ftock of provifion, do they tend to increafe the number of the people.*"—We are taught to fay of trade, "*that it maintains multitudes;*" but by what means does it maintain them, when it produces nothing upon which the fupport of human life depends?

pends?—In like manner with respect to foreign commerce; of that merchandise which brings the necessaries of life into a country, which imports, for example, corn, or cattle, or cloth, or fuel, we allow the tendency to advance happiness, because it increases the stock of provision by which the people are subsisted.—Here, therefore, as before, we may fairly ask, by what operation it is, that *foreign commerce*, which brings into the country not many articles of human subsistence, promotes the pleasures of human life?

Since the soil will maintain many more than it can employ, what must be done, supposing the country to be full with the remainder of the inhabitants? They who, by the rules of partition (and some such must be established in every country), are entitled to the land; and they who, by their labour upon the soil, acquire a right in its produce, will not part with their property for nothing; or rather, they will no longer raise from the soil what they can neither use themselves, nor exchange for what they want.—Or, lastly, if these were willing to distribute what they could spare of the provision which the ground yielded, to others who had no share or concern in the property or cultivation of it, yet still the most enormous mischiefs would ensue from great

numbers

numbers remaining unemployed.—*The idleneſs of one half of the community would overwhelm the whole with confuſion and diſorder.*—One only way preſents itſelf of removing the difficulty which this queſtion ſtates, and which is ſimply this; that they, whoſe work is not wanted, nor can be employed in the raiſing of proviſion out of the ground, convert their hands and ingenuity to the fabrication of articles which may gratify and requite thoſe who are ſo employed, or who, by the diviſion of lands in the country, are entitled to the excluſive poſſeſſion of certain parts of them.—By *this contrivance* all things proceed well.—The occupier of the ground raiſes from it the utmoſt that he can procure, becauſe he is repaid for what he can ſpare by ſomething elſe, which he wants, or with which he is pleaſed: the artiſt and manufacturer, though he have neither any property in the ſoil, nor any concern in its cultivation, is regularly ſupplied with the produce, becauſe he gives in exchange for what he ſtands in need of ſomething, upon which the receiver places an equal value: and the community is kept quiet, whilſt both ſides are engaged in their reſpective occupations.

It appears then, "THAT THE BUSINESS OF ONE HALF OF MANKIND IS TO SET THE OTHER HALF AT WORK;"

WORK;" that is, to provide articles, which, by tempting the desires, may stimulate the industry, and call forth the activity of those, upon the exertion of whose industry, and the application of whose faculties, the production of human provision depends.—A certain portion only of human labour is, or can be *productive*; the rest is *instrumental*—both *equally necessary*, though the one have no other object than to excite the other.

It appears also, that it signifies nothing as to the main purpose of trade, how superfluous the articles which it furnishes are; whether the want of them be real or imaginary; whether it be founded in nature or in opinion, in fashion, habit, or emulation: it is enough that they be actually desired and sought after.—Flourishing cities are raised and supported by trading in tobacco: popular towns subsist by the manufactory of ribbons.—A watch may be a very unnecessary appendage to the dress of a peasant, yet if the peasant will till the ground in order to obtain a watch, the true design of trade is answered; and the watch-maker, whilst he polishes the case, or files the wheels of his machine, is contributing to the production of corn as effectually, though not so directly, as if he handled the spade or held the plough.—The use of tobacco has been mentioned already, not only as an acknowledged superfluity, but as affording a remarkable example of the caprice of human appetite: yet, if the fisherman will ply his nets, or the mariner fetch rice from foreign countries, in order to procure to himself this indulgence, the market is supplied with two important articles of provision, by the instrumentality of a merchandise which has no other apparent use than the gratification of a vitiated palate.

But it may come to pass that the husbandman, land-owner, or whoever he be, that is entitled to the produce of the soil, will no longer exchange it for what the manufacturer has to offer.—He is already supplied to the extent of his desires.—For instance, he wants no more cloth; he will no longer therefore give the weaver corn, in return for the produce of his looms; but he would readily give it for *tea*, or for *wine*.—When the weaver finds this to be the case, he has nothing to do but to send *his cloth* abroad in *exchange* for *tea* or for *wine*, which he may barter for that provision which the offer of his cloth will no longer procure.—The *circulation* is thus revived; and the benefit of the discovery is, that whereas the number of weavers, who could find subsistence from their employment, was before limited by the consumption of cloth in the country, that number is now augmented in proportion to the demand for tea and for wine. —This is the principle of FOREIGN COMMERCE.—In the magnitude and complexity of the machine, the principle of motion is ſometimes loſt or unobſerved; but it is always ſimple and the ſame, to whatever extent it may be diverſified and enlarged in its operation.

The effect of trade upon agriculture, the proceſs of which we have been endeavouring to deſcribe, is viſible in the neighbourhood of trading towns, and in thoſe diſtricts which carry on a communication with the markets of trading towns.—The huſbandmen are buſy and ſkilful; the peaſantry laborious; the lands are managed to the beſt advantage, and double the quantity of corn or herbage (articles which are ultimately converted into human proviſion) raiſed from it, of what the ſame ſoil yields in remoter and more neglected parts of the country.—Wherever a thriving manufactory finds means to eſtabliſh itſelf, a new vegetation ſprings up around it.—I believe it is true that agriculture never arrives at any conſiderable, much leſs at its higheſt degree of perfection, where it is not connected with trade; that is, where the demand for the produce is not increaſed by the conſumption of trading cities.

It muſt be here however noticed, that we have all along conſidered the inhabitants of a country as maintained by the produce of the country: and that what we have ſaid is applicable with ſtrictneſs to this ſuppoſition alone.—The reaſoning, nevertheleſs, may eaſily be adapted to a different caſe; for when proviſion is not produced, but *imported*, what has been affirmed concerning proviſion, will be, in a great meaſure, true of that article, whether it be money, produce, or labour, which is exchanged for proviſion.—Thus, when the *Dutch* raiſe madder, and exchange it for corn; or when the people of *America* plant tobacco, and ſend it to *Europe* for cloth; the cultivation of madder and tobacco become as neceſſary to the ſubſiſtence of the inhabitants, and, by conſequence, will affect the ſtate of population in theſe countries as ſenſibly as the actual production of food, or the manufactory of raiment.—In like manner, when the ſame inhabitants of *Holland* earn money by the carriage of the produce of one country to another, and with that money purchaſe the proviſion from abroad, which their own land is not extenſive enough to ſupply, the increaſe or decline of this carrying trade will influence the happineſs of the people no leſs than ſimilar changes would do in the cultivation of the ſoil.

From the reaſoning that has been purſued, and the various conſiderations ſuggeſted in this ſection, a judgment may, in ſome ſort, be formed, how far regulations of *Law* are in their nature capable of contributing to the ſupport and advancement of happineſs.—I ſay *how far*: for, as in many ſubjects, ſo eſpecially in thoſe which relate to commerce, to plenty, and to riches, more is wont to be *expected* from laws, *than laws can do*.—*Laws* cannot regulate the wants of mankind, their mode of living, or their deſire of thoſe ſuperfluities which faſhion, more irreſiſtible than laws, has once introduced into general uſage, or, in other words, has erected into neceſſaries of life.—*Laws* cannot induce men to enter into marriages, when the expences of a family muſt deprive them of that ſyſtem of accommodation to which they have habituated their expectations.—*Laws*, by their protection, by aſſuring to the labourer the fruit and profit of his labour, may help to make a people induſtrious; but without induſtry the laws cannot provide either ſubſiſtence or employment; *Laws* cannot make corn grow without toil and care; or trade flouriſh without art and diligence.—*In ſpite of Laws*, the expert, laborious, honeſt workman will be employed, in preference to the lazy, the unſkilful, the fraudulent, and evaſive: and this is not more true of two inhabitants of the ſame village, than it is of the people of two different countries, which communicate either with each other, or with the rest of the world.—The natural basis of trade is rivalship of quality and price; or, which is the same thing, of skill and industry.—Every attempt to *force trade* by operation of law, that is, by compelling persons to buy goods at one market, which they can obtain cheaper and better from another, is sure to be either eluded by the quick-sightedness and incessant activity of private interest, or to be frustrated by retaliation.—One half of the commercial laws of many states are calculated merely to counteract the restrictions which have been imposed by other states.—Perhaps the only way in which the interposition of law is salutary in trade, is in the prevention of frauds.

The principal expedient to encourage *agriculture*, is *to adjust the laws of property*, as nearly as possible, to the following rules:—*First*, To give to the occupier all the power over the soil which is necessary for its perfect cultivation;—*Secondly*, To assign the whole profit of every improvement to the persons by whose activity it is carried on.

What we call property in land, as hath been observed above, is power over it.—Now it is indifferent to the public

public in whofe hands this power refides, *if it be rightly ufed:* it matters not to whom the land belongs, if it be well cultivated.—When we lament that great eftates are often united in the fame hand, or complain that one man poffeffes what would be fufficient for a thoufand, we fuffer ourfelves to be mifled by words.—The owner of ten thoufand pounds a year *confumes* little more of the produce of the foil than the owner of ten pounds a year. —*If the cultivation be equal, the eftate in the hands of one great lord affords fubfiftence and employment to the fame number of perfons as it would do if it were divided amongft a hundred proprietors.*—In like manner, we ought to judge of the effect upon the public intereft, which may arife from lands being holden by the king, or by the fubject; by private perfons, or by corporations; by lay men, or ecclefiaftics; in fee, or for life; by virtue of office, or in right of inheritance.—I do not mean that thefe varieties make no difference, but I mean, that all the difference they do make refpects the cultivation of the lands which are fo holden.

There exift in this country conditions of tenure, which condemn the land itfelf to perpetual fterility.— Of this kind is *the right of common,* which precludes each proprietor from the improvement, or even the conveni-

ent

ent occupation of his estate, without, what seldom can be obtained, the consent of many others.—This tenure is also usually embarrassed by the interference of *manerial* claims, under which it often happens that the surface belongs to one owner and the soil to another; so that neither owner can stir a clod without the concurrence of his partner in the property.—In many manors, the tenant is restrained from granting *leases* beyond a short term of years; which renders every plan of solid improvement impracticable.—In these cases the owner *wants*, what the first rule of rational policy requires, "*sufficient power over the soil for its perfect cultivation*." This power ought to be extended to him by some easy and general law of enfranchisement, partition, and enclosure; which, though compulsory upon the lord, or the rest of the tenants, *whilst it has in view the melioration of the soil*, and tenders an equitable compensation for every right that it takes away, is neither more arbitrary, nor more dangerous to the stability of property, than that which is done in the construction of roads, bridges, embankments, navigable canals, and indeed in almost every public work in which private owners of land are obliged to accept that price for their property which an indifferent jury may award.—*It may*

 here

here however be proper to observe, that although the inclosure of wastes and pastures be generally beneficial to population, yet the inclosure of lands in tillage, in order to convert them into pastures, is as generally hurtful.

But secondly, *agriculture* is *discouraged* by every constitution of landed property, which lets in those who have no concern in the improvement to a participation of the profit.—This objection is applicable to all such customs of *manors* as subject the proprietor, upon the death of the lord or tenant, or the alienation of the estate, to a fine apportioned to the improved value of the land.—But of all institutions which are in this way adverse to cultivation and improvement, none is so *noxious* as that of TITHES.—*A claimant here enters into the produce who contributed no assistance whatever to the production.—When years, perhaps, of care and toil have matured an improvement; when the husbandman sees new crops ripening to his skill and industry, the moment he is ready to put his sickle to the grain, he finds himself compelled to divide his harvest with a stranger.*—TITHES *are a tax not only upon industry, but upon that industry which feeds mankind; upon that species of exertion which it is the aim of all wise laws to cherish and promote; and to uphold and excite which, composes, as we have seen, the main benefit that the*

the community receives from the whole ſyſtem of trade, and the ſucceſs of commerce.—And, together with the more general inconveniency that attends the exaction of TITHES, *there is this additional evil, in the mode at leaſt according to which they are collected at preſent, that they operate as a bounty upon paſturage.—The burthen of the tax falls with its chief, if not with its whole weight, upon tillage; that is to ſay, upon that preciſe mode of cultivation, which, as hath been ſhewn above, it is the buſineſs of the ſtate to relieve and remunerate, in preference to every other *.*

* ARCHDEACON PALEY.

SECT.

www.ingramcontent.com/pod-product-compliance
Lightning Source LLC
Chambersburg PA
CBHW030824270326
41928CB00007B/879

* 9 7 8 3 3 3 7 0 6 9 3 2 2 *